KEVIN

My Memories

Gabrielle Kirby

Published by SOL Productions Ltd,.
Quarantine Hill, Wicklow Town,
Co. Wicklow, Ireland

ISBN 1-90171-234-6

Edited by Seamus Byrne
Graphic Design by Seamus Byrne
All Photographs by Servants of Love community
except...
P. 70 'Basking Shark', David Mark (Pixabay)
P. 78 'Periwinkle', Guttorm Flatabø (Wikimedia Commons)
P. 92 'Torshavn', Aline Dassel (Pixabay)

Dedicated to

All the members of Mary's Followers of the Cross, later called the Servants of Love, and to every person associated with us past, present and future.

And to Kevin's family, relations and friends in Ireland, Denmark and elsewhere.

Introduction

Kevin was extraordinary. He cared about everyone. He went out of his way to help others, but his love for God came first, then his neighbour. Kevin was different. He had a great mind. He saw things in a different light, which enabled him to follow his own star, irrespective of what others thought about him or what he was doing. He had a path that he wanted to take and he did everything in his power to make that work. When he had tried everything and he came up against a wall, he just changed direction and tried a new way or just tried something else. He never ever took 'no' for an answer. He just kept motoring through difficulties until he had success.

He was a happy man and saw the funny side of situations. Our lives with Kevin were at times hard, but always purposeful and joyous. We spent a lot of time laughing at all the funny situations we would get into, whether through contact work on the street, travelling to Fleadh Cheoils, evangelising in the Isle of Man or Courtown, sleeping rough in homemade sleeping bags or climbing snowy paths through the Dublin mountains to do penance to support our work on the street. It was a huge adventure from start to finish and so enjoyable, and we will always be grateful to Kevin for showing us how to live our lives to the fullest.

His passion was for the ordinary man in the street to dare to become a saint. A saint being a friend of God. A saint being a person who has good will and always makes an effort to put God first in absolutely everything they do, thereby giving great purpose to one's life. He always talked about how to become a saint. He loved to study the science of the saints and he had his favourites - St. Francis of Assisi, St. Therese of Lisieux, St. Philip Neri and many more. His favourite saying from the book 'The Family that Overtook Christ' was when the father told his sons that there was only one mistake you can make in life and that was 'not to become a saint'.

Gabrielle Kirby

Contents

Growing up in World War Two

Kevin (Nils) Jacobsen was born in Copenhagen, Denmark to Marie Holm and Arne Jacobsen in 1933. He was their second son. His brother, Jokum, was three years older than him.

'My early recollection of my mother is that she was a very caring and loving person who gave me a lot of affection. I think she liked me a lot; it must be what they call a fond mother's love. There was a woman who loved babies, but when she saw me she was speechless. My mother found that very amusing. My father was rather stern and a busy man. I seemed to annoy my brother a lot, as we were always fighting. He was three years older than me.'

Kevin with his mother

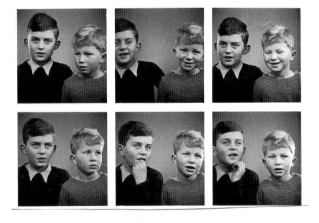

Kevin and Jokum (left)

Kevin used to tell us all about the things he got up to with his friends in the war years, mostly himself and his friend Alan Theusen. They made bombs and set them off on the wasteland near where they lived. They seemed to have had great fun at that because he was always telling the community about it.

He also learned to toughen up...

'I had a school pal and, whenever we did something wrong, we got punished by being slapped in the face, which happened quite often; either we were very bold or else the teacher on watch in the schoolyard had it in for us. My pal, who wore glasses, was so used to getting slapped that the minute the teacher would come over he would automatically take off his glasses, get the slap on one side, then turn his face and get slapped on the other side, shake his head and put back on the glasses, as if it was the most natural thing in the world. Which showed me how to deal with a hurt! But I'm afraid I was not so brave, as I was a spoiled child that usually would sulk after getting hurt.'

During the war, cigarettes were very hard to come by. Once, while in Copenhagen, both Jokum and Kevin were meeting up with their cousin, Jeffrey, in the English Hotel. Kevin loved to tell the story that while they were in the hotel with their cousin, both himself and Jokum went around the lobby collecting all the cigarette butts from the ashtrays to smoke later. Their cousin was very embarrassed!

The English Hotel

Having seen The Quiet Man

While still in Denmark, Kevin saw the film 'The Quiet Man'. It had a huge influence on him, reminding him strongly of time he had spent with his relations on the Faroe Islands when he was about fourteen years of age. He was very impressed with the simplicity of the peoples' lives. He came to realise that there was a whole world outside Denmark that he knew very little about. After seeing 'The Quiet Man' he decided to go to Ireland to see what it was like there. He didn't have much money so he hitched around the country living as simply as he could. For company he had a little kitten. To make sure the kitten wouldn't be taken from him as he passed through customs, he walked the kitten till it was very tired, then slipped it inside his jacket so the kitten would fall asleep and not wake up and give the game away. His kitten went everywhere with him. He really loved cats, but he was always talking about how selfish they were. If someone fed them a bit better than you, they were gone! He thought they were not a very loyal animal at all.

While in Dublin one day, studying his Danish/English dictionary, a homeless person who was sitting next to him said that he knew another Danish man living in Dublin and that he would bring him to meet him. Kevin decided to go with him. He followed him through the streets of Dublin. As they were getting into areas that looked a bit unusual to say the least, very poor areas, Kevin was getting a bit worried, wondering where the man was taking him. Anyway, they ended up in a home for homeless men called 'The Morning Star Hostel'. It was there he was introduced to Orla Knudsen, a fellow Dane, who was working in the Legion of Mary (a Roman Catholic lay organisation) house for the homeless in Rutland Street, Dublin. Kevin was very impressed with the work Orla did and the fact that he wasn't paid in any way for his work. He felt that the books he had been reading about heroes paled in comparison to what this man had given up to do this type of work. He would clean up after these men and sometimes vomit because of the state of the toilets he had to clean, and still he did it. This was the beginning of Kevin getting the Catholic faith.

Falling in love with Inishere

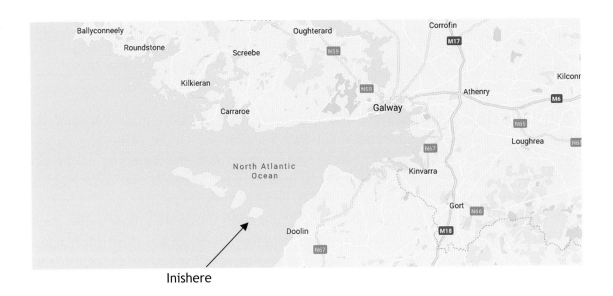

Inishere

Kevin with Orla Knudsen on Inishere, outside Kevin's house on the island.

Also in picture - Kevin's cat.

Orla told Kevin about Inishere, the smallest of the Aran Islands and how wonderful life was out there, and how different to life lived everywhere else. Kevin decided to make a journey out to see for himself. He was bowled over, not just by the island, but by the whole way of island life.

He decided he would like to stay in Inishere, but he needed money to do that, so he took a job on a Swedish boat that was travelling to China to pick up peanuts. He had many hair-raising experiences on that trip, not just the inclement weather, but with the ship's crew who liked to drink a lot. They knew that Kevin didn't drink, so they tried to steal his money to buy more of it. It took all his skill and ingenuity to hold on to his earnings!

He loved China, the simple way the people lived, and he also loved the way they used to eat their meals with chopsticks out of little bowls. (He incorporated the bowls and chopsticks into our community mealtimes for a while. They took some time to get used to!)

He met a lovely Chinese girl who had a long black plait. To try and put her off from having anything to do with sailors, he made an appointment with her, but didn't show up! He felt she needed to learn not to trust sailors.

Kevin was very impressed with stories of heroism. On the high seas he read a lot of books that really made an impression on him - 'The Brothers Karamazov' and 'Crime and Punishment' by Dostoevsky, for example.

When he eventually returned from China, he arrived at his mother's door with a huge Chinese hat on his head and on his feet he had two left shoes.

His mother was amazed and wanted to know what happened to the right shoe. He told her that when he was on his travels, he met a man on the street who had no left leg and he had an abundance of left shoes, so Kevin swapped his right shoe for one of his left shoes and came home from China wearing two left shoes!

After his long trip to China, he now had enough money to return to his beloved Inishere. He was so delighted to be back again on the island and took up exactly where he left off. The locals were very taken by him. He was vitally interested in everything they did, and they taught him not just English but Irish as well. In time, he developed his own version of the Irish language and Irish sayings! The locals took him in and generally treated him like one of their own. He became known as the 'Dane'. Later on, his family, his community (us), and visitors who in some way were related to him were all called the 'Danes'.

He loved the place so much that he even wore the traditional dress of the Aran men - the navy blue woollen shirt, tweed trousers, Crios (a Gaelic belt woven out of wool) and Pamputtees (shoes made out of cow skin).

Early Kevin

Later Kevin (in the movies)

He made his own trousers. He got a piece of tweed material, folded it in half and laid it on the ground. He got a piece of chalk, then lay down on the material and drew a mark around his legs, then cut out the material and sewed up the trousers. As his sister-in-law told me, he had a lot of experience putting lobster pots together - he just sewed up the trousers the same way he repaired the lobster pots. He then got a piece of rope and tied it around his waist to stop the trousers from falling down.

He made wonderful friends. After much soul searching he decided he would like to become a Catholic. Brid and Edward encouraged him to go to the priest. He used to go for lessons once a week and eventually decided to take the plunge and be received into the Catholic Church.

Brid and Edward

Brid and Edward Flaherty became his godparents. They remained friends with Kevin until they died. Edward passed away in 1980 and Brid in 2004.

Kevin's family, his mother, brother and friends all became regular visitors to Inishere while Kevin lived there. They all loved the place and returned many times for holidays. In fact, Kevin's mother, Marie, had taken a job in a house in Dublin looking after an elderly lady. She became known for her wonderful Danish cooking and also travelled around the world as companion to the lady.

When Kevin left Inishere he would always write to Brid, letting her know what was going on in his life. But, as he didn't know how to spell English and could only write phonetically anyway (Kevin was dyslexic), it was an extreme challenge to Brid to decipher what he had written. She told me that oftentimes she would be out in the fields and it would dawn on her some little thing she had been trying to figure out that Kevin had written. She always loved getting his letters, though.

Kevin tried his best to earn a living while on Inishere. He started fishing. He had learned a lot from the fishermen who used to put out longlines near his summer home in Gudmindrup Lyng, Sealand, Denmark. He had watched the fishermen digging for worms and putting them on their hooks, setting out the lines from their boats, returning in the evening to collect the fish and eventually coming to his summer home to sell the fish they had caught.

Summer Home in Gudmindrup

Kevin started fishing for eels on the lake in Inishere. He got the local boat builder to make him a small one-man currach. The traditional Aran Islands fishing boat is larger and it takes three men to lift it, but Kevin wanted to be able to lift his currach on his own. He also created a little harbour for the currach on the lake. He used to tie up the currach in his little harbour and then, at nighttime, go with one of his local friends, John Kevin Conneely, with a torch, looking for worms which they used as bait for his hooks.

**The Lake
on Inishere**

**Kevin in his
one-man Currach**

One pitch-dark night, as he was out looking for worms, suddenly he felt an arm go around his shoulder. He nearly jumped out of his skin with the fright, but it turned out to be a blackberry bush that had caught on his jumper and held like an arm around his shoulder. He loved telling us that story.

When he caught the eels he would smoke them in a smoking kiln which he built himself. He sent off the smoked eels to Billingsgate, London for sale. The Naomh Éanna, the Galway-Aran supply boat, would take the eels to Galway and they were shipped on from there to London.

He made quite a living from eel fishing, but it still wasn't enough for him to survive. With a very heavy heart he left the island and moved to Galway. He started fishing on the boats there. Trawling was the traditional way of catching fish and he got a job on one of the local trawlers. He would get up at 4am in the morning and work on the boat all day until he got back to his gypsy-style caravan which was parked down by the Galway docks. He found Galway very lonely in comparison to life on Inishere. On Inishere, there was always a house to visit for a cup of tea and a chat, whereas in Galway he was all on his own.

**Visiting with friends
on Inishere**

Kevin became very interested in the Cistercian monks and their way of life, and especially in the monastery in Mount Melleray, County Waterford. He visited all the different monasteries several times, and loved the life so much that he decided to join and become a monk. But when he had a talk with a spiritual director, he was told that it wasn't God's will for him to become a monk but to go and get married. Very disheartened, he returned again to Galway.

He decided to join the Legion of Mary, a Catholic lay evangelistic organisation. It was while doing Legion work in the local hospital that he met Mary Dooley. She was a patient suffering from TB. He loved talking with her. They had so much in common, especially spiritually, and they loved discussing all aspects of the faith together. They would talk for hours and hours on end. Mary eventually got better, so they decided to get married. They went to Mount Melleray monastery for their honeymoon. So began his very happily married life in Galway, fishing, doing Legion of Mary work and bringing up their five sons - Louis, Bernard, Joseph, Mark and Philip. Both Mary and Kevin were very active in the Legion of Mary in Galway. When they married first they didn't have a house to live in, only Kevin's little boat which he kept down at the Claddagh. Mary told me how easy it was to get Louis to go asleep as he seemed to love the movement of the boat swaying in the water. Eventually they moved into a small little flat in Galway. Working the trawlers was very hard, so Kevin teamed up with a fisherman from Gleninagh and they fished lobsters together in nearby Ballyvaughan and the Black Head area.

The
Wedding

Kevin and Mary's Flat

Later, they moved into a small house near the pier in Barna, where again he fished for lobsters. He made his own lobster pots and was well able to repair them because of all the experience he had gained in Inishere. He also worked with a man in Galway for a long time, on the trawlers.

The house in Barna

Cold smoking mackerel

Kevin introduced the technique of cold smoking mackerel to Ireland. It hadn't been known before he started it up. He made a huge smoking kiln for himself, but later sold it to a fishmonger in Galway. It was still in use twenty years after he made it and could still be there for all I know. When he moved to Dublin, he made another smoking kiln. He would buy salmon, smoke them and sell them to a fish shop in Grafton street.

Move to Dublin and the Legion of Mary

Legion of Mary statue of Mary

After much thought, Mary and Kevin decided to move to Dublin to see if they could spread the faith there. They found an apartment in Stillorgan and joined the Dublin Legion of Mary. Kevin made quite an impression in the Legion in Dublin. After setting up his first praesidium (the Legion of Mary was styled on the Roman Army, hence the name 'praesidium' which means a group meeting of like-minded individuals), the attendance doubled and trebled in a very short time, so that he had to set up several praesidia.

The work that Kevin did in the Legion was called 'street work' or 'contact work'. It involved approaching young people on the street or any public place and trying to interest them in loving God. It was in the museum in Dublin that I first met him. This was the way most of the present members of The Servants of Love met Kevin, through interest in helping others or themselves to a greater love for God. Kevin then moved to Hughes Road North, Walkinstown as the apartment in Stillorgan wasn't big enough for all the people that were coming to his meetings.

Although Kevin had a lot of success setting up new praesidia and gathering a vast amount of new members, when he would split his praesidium in two, over time the new group, not being exposed to his strong evangelical spirit, would begin to falter. They would change the work to perhaps something less challenging, and then the members would lose interest and leave that praesidium.

Kevin was a trained carpenter/cabinet maker, so, in Dublin, he started off a cabinet-making business. He was much sought after as a Danish cabinet maker and many rich people brought him in to fit out their kitchens. Ib Jorgensen hired him to fit out his kitchen. He didn't really like cabinet making, one reason being it was very hard for him to get paid, especially from people who had plenty of money. They were always looking for reasons not to pay him. They would try to find things wrong with the work he did and then delay payment until he fixed it up. He had many trying clients and the day he got out of that business was one of his fondest memories.

I suppose because he was a very spiritual man, he found it hard to see the purpose of worrying about something small that was out of line or perhaps didn't have *exactly* the right colour. Whereas this may have been a priority for some people, it was not a priority for Kevin.

Kevin held his Legion praesidium meeting every Tuesday night at 8pm in his house on Hughes Road North, Walkinstown. When we invited people we met on the street to the meeting, they would come to his carpenters workshop at the back of his house. He would throw a huge cover over his band saw, put the statue of Our Lady, cloth, candles, etc. on top of that and the meeting would commence. It was there that I first went to a Legion of Mary meeting led by Kevin. It was very impressive; there were so many young people and the way they said the Rosary was very moving. There was always a big crowd at the meeting and afterwards we would have a cup of tea and a chat with whoever would come as a visitor. It was terrific; we were meeting new people all the time. The numbers eventually became too big for the carpenters workshop, so Mary allowed us to move the meeting into the house.

One thing that stands out in my mind in relation to Kevin was his disregard for what people thought about him. I'm not sure if it's a Danish trait or was just in Kevin's personality. One aspect of that was, for comfort's sake, Kevin used to wear Scholl sandals all the time. Even when it rained he would have them on. So as not to get his feet wet, he would put plastic bags over his sandals and an elastic band over each plastic bag to keep the rain out. It looked so funny and also embarrassing if you were with him walking down Grafton Street to get to the place where you would begin the contact work.

After I joined the community, I agreed to go on contact work, to try it out, to see would I like it. I was amazed when I arrived at the arranged meet-up spot in Grafton Street because nearly all the boys in the group had beards and, as well as that, they all had motor bikes! I thought to myself, 'How cool is that! There are actually boys in the world who want to love God. They have beards and motorbikes as well!' After a second's more reflection I thought to myself, 'I'm in!' There was no looking back after that!

Dynamic Evangelisation

The Legion of Mary requirement was a commitment of two hours work per week plus attendance at a weekly praesidium meeting. Kevin worked every night from 7.30pm to 10pm, a meeting once a week and also did what is known as the 'Sunday Trip'. The 'Sunday Trip' was actually Kevin's own invention, and, as far as I know, is still practised by the Legion of Mary to this day. He described it as 'a day given to God'. It started very early on Sunday morning at the Pillar Café on O'Connell Street. After meeting up, we would disperse for work, in pairs, contacting people until 5pm, with a break for lunch at 1pm, ending up in Kevin's house at 8pm for what we called the 'Sunday Night Discussion'. Kevin's group got so big that he was constantly expanding his premises. He eventually knocked down the wall between his dining room and sitting room to accommodate all those who wanted to attend his meetings.

To start off the discussion, Kevin would bring up a subject on some relevant spiritual point and then throw it out for people to comment on. The discussion was then in progress, becoming usually 'heated' and followed, after about two hours, by the regular cup of tea and a biscuit.

We came into conflict with some other members of the Legion of Mary because they didn't seem to understand or approve of the amount of time we were putting into the work and the areas we were working in. We were doing much, much more than the regulation two hours, but we were also working outside our 'area'. Each praesidium is assigned an area to do the work they are appointed to do. Kevin always chose places where most young people congregated, hence the city centre. But the Legion authorities thought we should do the work in our assigned area, which was Thomas Street. We had tried the pubs in Thomas Street many times, but at times there would be only one person in any pub and the street in the evening was very quiet. There just wasn't the same amount of people, especially young people, to talk to. However, Kevin agreed to do what was asked of him; so once a week we would do our two hours work in Thomas Street on Friday or Saturday night. And then the rest of the week we would work in Dublin city centre, on our own time, as it were. That worked out very well. The Legion authorities were happy we were doing what they wanted and we were happy because we could dedicate the rest of our time to the area where there was a good flow of young people.

Around that time, Kevin became very interested in the power of friendship as an encouragement to become a saint. He felt that everyone needed encouragement to overcome their weaknesses. Becoming a saint was something that Frank Duff, the founder of the Legion of Mary, felt was open to every person, no matter who they were. It was something the ordinary person on the street could aspire to if they were given enough positive encouragement. This was something that Kevin was discovering more and more all the time. He often gave the example of his own case. He hated brushing his teeth and no matter how many times he was reminded, he never did, until one of the girls in the group said to him one day, 'You have lovely teeth. Did you ever think of brushing them?' From that day on he never missed a brushing!

Seeds of Community Life

Kevin suggested to a few of the members of the group that we should try to move into an apartment together. Gerry Finnegan, Maureen Kehoe and myself set about looking up ads for apartments. Eventually, we found a suitable one in Rathmines and moved into that. It was tough going at the beginning. Getting used to living with more than one person was a real challenge, but we were supported by Kevin all through the time we lived there. We eventually came up with the idea of a weekly meeting, which Kevin attended. At the meeting, we would iron out any grievances that developed in the past week. We eventually came up with a set of guidelines so that living together was enjoyable rather than a burden. Kevin was at the helm of every move we made. He was excited at the possibility of forming a community of young people dedicated to becoming a saint through living a life of simplicity and spreading the Gospel message in this new way.

I left my job as an apprentice dress designer and got a job working at 'Dorothy Pinnocks', a clothing factory which was just about 15 mins up the road from the apartment. Sometimes, if we were having a meeting in the apartment, Kevin would collect me from work on his motorbike and give me a lift home. When the girls I worked with saw him waiting outside they would jeer me the next day, or run back and tell me, 'Your boyfriend is waiting outside for you.' I didn't particularly like it, so I warned Kevin to wait around the corner so no one could see him. He also used to wear a funny-looking motorbike helmet, which I hated, so when I saw him around the corner with the helmet on, I gave in to human respect, hopped on the bus when it arrived and left him waiting for me. He eventually got the message and arrived at the apartment unperturbed.

I eventually was let go from my job in 'Dorothy Pinnocks' for talking instead of churning out a thousand items. It was a blessing in disguise. I set up my own dress making business in the apartment. Kevin bought me my first sewing machine, which I still have and still works! I put an ad in the paper and I was on my bike. Once I got business I was then in a position to pay him back.

'The Chart' system

He brought in a system called 'The Chart'. Everyone who wanted had a partner and, once a week, you would meet and discuss what you wanted to achieve for the week. You then kept a chart of your week. You would have various things on the chart e.g. Daily Mass, Confession, Aspirations (short, repeated prayers) and then things that you were trying to overcome like giving up cigarettes, being nice to somebody you didn't like or whatever was your particular weakness.

At your weekly meeting you would show your chart to your partner, and vice versa, and give each other much needed encouragement to continue for another week. You usually had a partner for a couple of months, then you would get a new partner. It was a terrific system and worked very well. The whole system was centred around loving God more and also becoming a saint. It was always great when there was a change of partner. You would go somewhere and have a small celebration, which was always enjoyable.

Kevin liked to go wherever there was a gathering of young people. In the summer time we went to a beach, often to Seapoint where Kevin's mother, Marie, lived. When Kevin moved to Dublin, Marie also decided to move from Denmark. We would do the contact work on the beach and when we had a break he would go and pay her a visit.

Marie

Summertime was also great for music and beer festivals. Kevin would get all the boys together, all those that had motorbikes. Each bike would carry a passenger and off we would go to the festival. In 1968 we went to a Fleadh Cheoil in Cashel.

Ballinasloe 1968

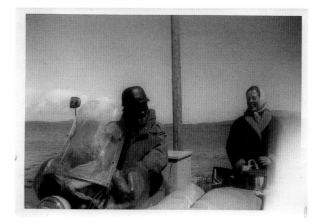

Ballyvaughan 1971

For that particular one, Kevin invented a waterproof covering for each sleeping bag. The head of each bag would be faced inwards so all the heads would be together. Then he set up his plastic covering over all the heads of the sleepers so that the rain would fall on the end of each sleeping bag and not on the head. Each sleeping bag had its own plastic bag. It worked like a dream and Kevin was really happy that his invention had worked.

Cashel Waterproof Covering

In 1969 we decided to go to Courtown to do Legion work. We called to the local priest and he gave us an old barn and the upstairs of a shed. The boys stayed in the barn and the shed upstairs, which was very cosy, was for the girls. The barn previously was home to cows; there were old hay stalls all around the walls. The boys filled up the stalls with hay, then put their sleeping bags on top of the hay and had a wonderful night's sleep. It happened that while the boys were getting their 'bedroom' ready they disturbed some bats that suddenly flew out. One boy commented, 'Oh we have a bat room!' The central area in the barn was also where we had our meals. The table consisted of old timber crates that were lying around the barn, but did wonderfully as our meal table. There were about 15 of us altogether.

Courtown 1969

We went to the beach every day, armed with a bunch of Miraculous Medals, and tried to interest the young people in talking about God. At night time we went into the pubs and talked to them there. It was a wonderful time. It wasn't long before everyone in town was wearing a Miraculous Medal. We would even have people come up to us on the street and in the pubs, asking for a medal for themselves or their friends. There was a great spirit of camaraderie. It was a very special time.

We used to go to Mass in the morning and then have breakfast, then do our work on the beach, the street or anywhere there was anyone to talk to, till lunchtime.

We used to have our lunch on the grass here, long before it was all built up.

Lunch break was relaxing on the bank of the river in the sun eating burgers and chips. When lunch was over we would go back to the beach, cafés or wherever we would meet people. I remember once being on work with Kevin when he suddenly felt a migraine headache coming on. I remember him trying to use his inhaler to ward it off, but he couldn't get it to work. He even tried to clear it by washing it in a puddle on the street. Eventually, he had to go back to the barn and try to sleep it off. He had to stay in the dark as the light only made it worse. He suffered a lot from migraines down through the years, but in the latter years they eased off a lot and they would only be very mild.

Isle of Man

In the summer of 1971 we decided to go a bit further afield - the Isle of Man. We took our sleeping bags with us, together with the waterproof covering. When we arrived in the Isle of Man we had to find a place to sleep as it was late at night. We did our best to find a good location. Eventually we came upon a field, pitched our sleeping bags and tried to get some sleep.

Preaching

In the morning we moved on to a better area, to where there were more people. But first, something to eat. We found a bakery. Buns were the order of the day for breakfast. Later on, Kevin went to a scrap yard and bought a pan and a primus stove. We set up in a shelter near the beach and that was where we had breakfast every morning before we started out contacting on the beach. The people were very friendly and welcoming. It was there too that Kevin got the idea to actually preach on the street. He was the one to start it off. He found a street that was particularly busy and stood up and started speaking. Then another boy volunteered to try it out. We thought they were very courageous! None of the girls undertook that particular operation.

After we returned home from the Isle of Man, Kevin kept up the idea of preaching on the street. He even made a platform that you could wheel into place. You stood up on it and you could also rest your arms on the front of it. The very first time I had the courage to get up and preach, a man came along and presented me with a bottle of champagne. I was thrilled! Kevin also used to bribe us with an ice cream cone if we did it. As a result, there were many willing to give it a go! We eventually got used to preaching and added that to our repertoire.

Kevin had a priest friend, Fr. Bradshaw, who was stationed in Tipperary and was in charge of Seminarian Formation. As part of their curriculum, when they came to Dublin for a few days, they had a meeting with a former atheist. So Kevin, the former atheist, would entertain them in his house in Walkinstown. It was always extremely interesting to listen to the discussions that went on between Kevin and the seminarians. They would also try out the contact work on the street and in the pubs. They were extremely willing to learn and also great fun to be with.

Kevin was invited to give a talk in Maynooth to the students there. That too was really interesting, but even more interesting was the fact that in the middle of his talk a little mouse appeared and the students' attention went onto the mouse. But Kevin continued his talk. The mouse didn't bother him at all.

One Fleadh Cheoil we attended was in Ballinasloe, Co. Galway. Up on the motorbikes and off we went for a weekend of fun. We pitched our tent on the bank of the river near the local church. It was a perfect location; being very close to the church we could get to Mass, no bother. It wasn't long before we were joined by a lot of other campers. At the tent next to us, a group of boys took out their frying pan and threw on a heap of sausages. To make the fire a bit stronger they heaped on some petrol and the fire was blazing! Kevin wasn't a bit impressed; it wasn't long before we were packing up and moving on to find a quieter, more suitable location, without the threat of being burnt alive in our tent! Kevin made all the hard decisions. For the rest of us, it was all fun. We were happy to move on and find a new place. It was all excitement for us!

Another tent experience we had was at a Fleadh Cheoil north of Dublin. As it was nearly the end of the summer and the weather was a little chilly, Kevin got the bright idea to call to a local farmer and see if he would supply us with one or two bales of hay. When bedtime came and we had done our day's work talking to people about God, we would have our supper and then pile into the tent and get into our sleeping bags. Then Kevin began to push in the loose hay on top of us. The idea was that the hay would keep us lovely and warm. Luckily, I had a spot at the exit, so I could breathe, because the hay was very dusty. But one of the girls at the far end of the tent got a bit worried, so she struggled her way out of the tent and went off to get herself a B & B for the night. She just couldn't take the hay; it was just too much for her. I remember I had a blanket over my sleeping bag, and I was picking hay seeds out of the blanket forever after that.

At another Fleadh Cheoil, Antoinette found a huge bundle of money. We made it known that we had found it and the owner soon came to collect it. I think maybe it was money for drugs.

Whirlwind Evangelisation

In March 1971, Kevin's father died and left him some money. At first he decided he was going to open a second-hand motorbike shop, but then, after much reflection with Mary, he announced that he would buy a van, kit it out for living in and we could leave the flat and our jobs and go to live in the van. The purpose of living in the van was poverty and it would be possible to go all over the country with a view to saving the faith in Ireland. It was an exciting and very fearful time for us, not so much for Kevin. But I'm sure he had some fears, too. We liked the idea of doing the work full time, but having to leave our apartment in Rathmines and our jobs was a huge challenge.

For our new home, then, we lived in a small blue van which Kevin kitted out with sleeping quarters, much like a mobile home, but not as posh. He made a timber box which sat on the top of the van, its full length. This compartment was the sleeping accommodation for the boys. It had an opening at both ends for access, which could also be kept open at night for air. To get up to the bed, the boys had to climb up with the aid of a pole every night. The girls slept in the van itself. As there were only a few of us in the beginning it was quite comfortable.

It was around that time that we decided to go vegetarian. I distinctly remember the meals, especially the dinner. It was so bland! Rice and vegetables, or vegetables and potatoes. We used to cook our meals in the blue van on the floor, on a gas ring. Not much health and safety rules, then! Anyhow, we survived. It was good fun and a great experience. We were totally supported by all the spiritual discussions we had at mealtimes about becoming a saint and loving God more. We travelled all over Ireland, evangelising. Dublin, Kerry, Offaly, Limerick and Cork are some of the places that come to mind.

On one of our trips to the Kilkenny Beer Festival, we were parked in a car park convenient to where the festival was taking place. We were actually parked right beside somebody's motorbike. One of the lads happened to be sick at the time, so he didn't go out on the street work. Staying back to have a rest, in the timber 'bedroom' on top of the van, he was awakened from his sleep by a man cursing and swearing, who didn't know he was being observed from above. Somebody had stolen the carburettor from his motorbike and he was absolutely livid. He literally did a dance after he made the discovery.

While in Kerry on Legion work one year, we met the canon of a church who invited Kevin to dinner with some other priests in the region. Before the dinner, the canon warned Kevin that he wasn't to talk about God to the other priests as this wouldn't go down well. Kevin's passion was always to talk about God any chance he got, and he thought this highly unusual, but he kept his word and did as he was told.

While we continued our whirlwind evangelisation, speaking to people, preaching and holding our meetings, new problems arose with Legion authorities and conflict started again. The Legion authorities said that Legion meetings should be in a designated Legion house, instead of in Kevin's home. Being in Kevin and Mary's home made it very easy for Mary to attend the meetings and discussions, because their kids were still small and they would have required a babysitter if the meeting was elsewhere. Kevin was also realising that the Legion didn't offer the facility for the kind of full-time evangelisation work we were doing. He reflected on what was happening and thought it was time to do something different.

Mary's Followers of the Cross

The secret of love lies in loving.

Kevin Jacobsen

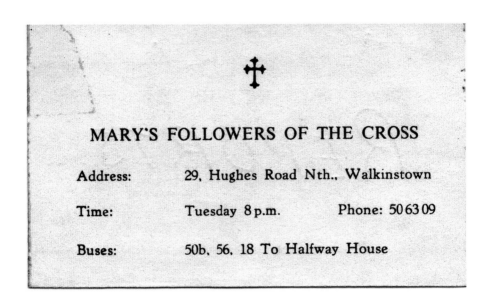

MARY'S FOLLOWERS OF THE CROSS

Address:	29, Hughes Road Nth., Walkinstown
Time:	Tuesday 8 p.m. Phone: 50 63 09
Buses:	50b, 56, 18 To Halfway House

Address Card with time of meeting

Kevin was good friends with Frank Duff, the founder of the Legion of Mary. We went to see him and told him what was happening and our plans to form our own group, but still evangelise on the street. Frank would have preferred if we had stayed in the Legion, but was very supportive and encouraging and told us to continue to come and visit him every now and then.

And so we had our first meeting of the new group, 'Mary's Followers of the Cross', on the 14th of December 1971, in Kevin and Mary's house in Walkinstown. It was a very exciting time for all the members. Essentially, we were doing the same work on the street as we were doing in the Legion of Mary, but we had much more scope and the sky was the limit.

After living in the small, blue van for about a year, Kevin eventually got rid of it and invested in a brand new Commer van, which was much bigger than the original one. Kevin's first job was to insulate it. He covered the outside with one inch thick aeroboard, then a layer of canvas and, on top of that, a layer of tar for waterproof purposes. The inside walls of the van were covered with carpet. It turned out very well and it was lovely and warm inside, even in the winter, which was good, because we had to live in it. As Kevin was a cabinet maker, he kitted it out with a table, sink, seating and sleeping accommodation for at least 18 people, and a little pedal organ for accompaniment for singing the Psalms.

New home -
Commer van

On the side of the van we had written 'Help save the faith in Ireland'. We travelled up and down the country in 'The Black Van', as we used to call it, working in whatever town we arrived in and, with the use of a loudspeaker system, preaching the faith as we drove around. When we used the loudspeaker, as we passed through the countryside, the cows never failed to run towards the van and the sheep ran further away. It was a very wonderful time; we were always on the move, going here, there and everywhere.

In Dublin, during the week, we would work on the streets - Grafton Street, Henry Street, O'Connell Street - stopping young people and asking them if they would be interested in loving God. We used to meet every night at 8pm in Westmoreland Street, outside Kingstons, a clothes shop for men that had a terrific doorway for meeting up. There we would say a prayer and go out in twos to the local pubs or just work on the streets stopping people, mostly young people, and asking them if they were interested in loving God. Most people were very nice. Some nights were great, other nights not so great. We just did the work and then let God take care of the rest.

Meeting up outside Kingstons

We would meet at the end of the night in the van and have a chat over a cup of tea, and each person would say how the night worked out for them. Then we would drive home to Walkinstown and our van would be parked in the laneway at the back of Kevin's house. We would sing the Psalms and go to bed. The beds in the Black Van consisted of the boys lying on the floor in sleeping bags and then planks would be laid out halfway up the van, making a separate floor, for the girls. I can't remember if we got up at night to say the Rosary or was that a later inspiration. So as not to waste time when travelling home, we would put the kettle on the cooker, somebody would hold the kettle in place and, so as not to get scalded by an unexpected stepping on the breaks, we put a baby's teat on the spout. It looked hilarious, but did the job.

Meeting after work, Sept. 1972 Black Van

At the weekends we would go away to a holiday resort and approach people everywhere we met them - on the beach, in their caravans, in the pubs, in all public places - offering them the chance of loving God and also a chance to wear the Miraculous Medal. Kevin was unstoppable. Sometimes we went further afield. We visited the west of Ireland and all the little places that Kevin had fished from. We visited Ballyvaughan, where Kevin began his fishing career, and dropped into Gleninagh to see Kevin's old lobster-fishing friend. Kevin parked his van outside the man's house and went in to pay him and his wife a visit. They were delighted to see him again, as it had been years since they had seen him last. We also stopped at the viewing point at Black Head, which is the closest you can get to a proper view of Inishere. I think the sight must have put a longing on Kevin to return to his beloved island. He had often said, though, that he wouldn't like to return in case his beautiful image and memories of Inishere would be shattered.

But in December 1973, Kevin took the plunge and we travelled out to Inishere to celebrate Christmas there. Kevin was never a fan of a commercial Christmas, which was probably one of the reasons he wanted to go to Inishere. We stayed in a cottage belonging to Brid, Kevin's godmother. I can't remember much of what we did at that time except we talked a lot about God and went for long walks. For our evening meal we had local dried fish and homegrown potatoes given to us by the locals. The same, simple fare every day. It was wonderful. 19 of us stayed in the little cottage. It was so homely and cute.

Christmas at Brid's Cottage

The Mark System

The community was very much a part of Kevin and Mary's family. We were all in it together. I knew the family from the time the kids were quite young; the oldest, Louis, being 10 or 11, the youngest, Philip, just one year old.

Kevin and Mary had a great system, called the Mark System. They never, ever physically punished their children, got annoyed or angry with them. Each child had their name on a piece of paper and when any one of them did something that was considered wrong or naughty, they got a 'mark', and when the marks accumulated to a certain number, they would get a day in their bedroom or some such punishment. They could do whatever they wanted in their room but they couldn't leave it. It was a great incentive for them not to fight or argue with their brothers (they were 5 boys!). They weren't allowed to grumble about their punishment either or they would get another mark. They were also allowed to work off their marks by doing something good or kind for their neighbour.

As far as I could see they were really happy kids, always laughing and enjoying life, always working on something, inventing things, making things work, or just helping out in their neighbours' garages. Down the back lane there was a panel beater and the older boys enjoyed helping out there.

Kevin, Mary
and the boys

The Mountain Trip

Kevin had the bright idea that we needed to do some penance. He thought that the work on the street needed a background of prayer and penance, so he started off what came to be known as the Mountain Trip. I can't remember now if this was once a week or once a month. What it consisted of was gathering at Kevin's house in Walkinstown after work in the pubs on Saturday night, around 11pm. We would have a cup of tea and something to eat, then all take off for the Dublin Mountains on motorbikes, or if someone was lucky enough to have a car we would go in that as well. It was entirely voluntary, but pretty much all of us did the trip every time it was on. We would leave the motorbikes outside the pub at the bottom of the mountain, and begin the walk from there, up past the Hell Fire Club, till we got to the top. Then we would make our way down again. We started off saying the Rosary on the way up, and then maintained silence until we got to the top. Once we got to the top, we would be able to talk on the way down. In the summer months it would be quite warm and also beautiful, but a litter harder in the winter, especially when it rained. But when it was snowing it was magical, nothing short of absolutely fabulous. Kevin invented rain gear for us, as funds were tight. He bought plastic, cut out a full length back and front, folded it over and melted the side edges together with an iron. I cut out a hole for the head and sewed in a long zip in the front which you could do up for yourself from the inside. It didn't have any sleeves, Each person got one of these to take with them, so when it started raining, we hauled out our 'rain gear'. Sometimes cars would pass us out when we had the plastic bags on. We looked hilarious in them and probably very strange, because a little later the police would arrive having gotten reports that 'zombies' were heading in the direction of the Dublin Mountains. The police would stop and chat to find out what we were doing. When we told them we were praying and doing penance, they wished us good luck and waved us on our way. Eventually, before our future trips, we would call up the Gardai and tell them our plans. They were delighted to be informed, so they could appease the worried people who might telephone in.

When we came down from the mountain, which would be about 7am on Sunday morning, we would go into the Dominican Church in Tallaght for Mass. We were not allowed to sit down, because as soon as we sat down we would fall asleep instantly. So we always stood at the back. It was fun trying to keep our eyes open, because once you come into a warm place, having been out in the cold for so long, you just drop off to sleep immediately. After Mass, we would make our way home and have a wonderful sleep!

Bow Lane, Dublin - 1972

All of us who are weak

are strong together.

Kevin Jacobsen

Because we had so many lay members - people who wanted to have a day job but were also interested in community living and dedicating their lives to God - Kevin bought a place in Dublin city centre called Bow Lane (now renamed Beaux Lane), very close to Whitefriar Street Church. It was originally an athletic club. It was a very poor area then, surrounded by flats, and the kids from the flats were always up to mischief. They tried to burn down our premises several times! If you left a window open, they would throw in burning papers, hoping for the best. The fires did a small amount of damage, but nothing major, thank God. We also had to make special timber coverings for the windows of the Black Van, to prevent the kids from throwing rocks at the windows. When we would all pile into the van to go on work, the kids would all hop on the back of the van to get a jaunt, which was very dangerous. So one of us was assigned to keep a look out so that wouldn't happen.

One memory from Bow Lane was how cold it was in winter. Some of the boys found it really hard, so they would gather up all their coats and any spare clothes and put them on top of their blankets to try to keep warm at night.

At that stage, we were rising in the middle of the night to say the Rosary and sing the Psalms. To stay awake we walked around as we prayed. There was a basin of cold water on a nearby table and, if you were falling asleep, the person in charge would give you a tip on the shoulder and you would have to throw some water on your face. It was a terrible experience. I didn't like it at all!

Because it was a former athletic club, there was athletic equipment left behind. We used to have great fun swinging out of the wires and bars, and also trying our hand at boxing the hanging speed ball. We had great fun. It was so central, really handy to go to Mass in the morning in Whitefriars Street Church and close to the city areas we worked in, e.g. Grafton Street, O'Connell Street, etc.

Kevin was gradually encouraging us to be more frugal, especially in our diet. So, bread-wise, we were restricted to one slice per meal. But because by nature we are so attached to food and survival in general, there used to be all sorts of shenanigans going on. You could have one slice, but you would pile it high with whatever you could find so it looked like the Eiffel Tower. There was just no end of material you could pile onto your one slice. The bread at that time was cooked in a roasting pot. It usually came out quite heavy. We called it 'lead bread' but it was delicious and also healthy. It was a great favourite, and one of the boys had a great touch at making it.

So, Kevin came up with the idea of measuring out our food. We called it 'The Food Grade'. For breakfast, we were allowed an egg and 1 slice of toast. 11 o'clock, 1 slice of bread and an eggcup full of nuts and seeds. Lunch was a salad and a slice of bread, and 4pm, 1 slice of bread with leeks and tomatoes on it, and a half apple. Dinner was potatoes or rice, and vegetables. On Fridays, it was just rice for dinner, as a form of penance.

At times, when you were out evangelising, you were allowed to go into a café for a cup of tea and a snack. But Seamus remembers going in with one of the other 'Followers' who said he was starving, and then ordered a huge dinner for himself. Seamus was amazed!

Another of our favourite drinks was Complan. If you were hungry and cold, to have a cup of Complan was just the job to hit the spot, especially if you could get two dollops of Complan into your cup without anyone noticing. That would be heaven. Because we were always hungry, we really enjoyed our food, so a cup of Complan added enormously to our happiness until our next meal. Yes, Complan was definitely a highlight of our meal day!

In Bow Lane, we often had visitors come to stay with us to experience our lifestyle. Michaela had a friend from Denmark, Paul Simon, who came and stayed with us for a few days. We normally all slept in our clothes on the floor in the same dorm. On his first night with us, he got up just as we were saying the Rosary. He had just his underwear and short coat on and walked through us to go down to use the toilet. Kevin made a beeline after him with his trousers, requesting that he put them on! We laughed a lot about that afterwards. One day, as Paul was out exploring the city, he was crossing O'Connell Bridge when a small Traveller boy came up to him offering him a watch. Paul replied with 'No thanks'. The boy continued to follow him, holding up the watch and saying something. Paul, despite his good English, couldn't quite understand. Paul kept insisting he had a watch and didn't want another one. When he got back to Bow Lane, he realised the watch that the boy was offering him was his own. He wasn't aware that it had fallen off his wrist and the boy kept trying to give it to him! We had a great laugh at that, and Paul always liked to tell that story afterwards.

We still held our meetings in Walkinstown once a week, which were open to the public, and the members met every night in Westmoreland Street to do the work on the street. The work consisted of direct preaching or standing on the streets, or going into pubs or any public place where young people gathered, always trying to engage them in conversation about loving God.

**About to go on
contact work
in Dublin**

We eventually seemed to have got through most of the people in Dublin, because not so many were stopping to talk anymore. We were thinking that maybe it was time to move on. But Kevin wasn't as free as the rest of us; he had Mary and their five children to consider. But Mary was always a huge supporter of whatever Kevin undertook. She always did the work on the street and, of course, opened her home to weekly meetings and the huge amount of people coming and going. She often had people staying with her long term, too, who had nowhere else to stay. Kevin would bring them home and she would take care of them. But Kevin was always looking ahead and always tuned into what God wanted him to do.

While doing the work at the music festivals, we met quite a lot of really friendly people from Cork. So Kevin thought of setting up in Cork to see if there might be any better interest there among the young people.

Blackrock Road, Cork - 1974

Our new house in Cork city

After much prayer and recollection, Kevin wrote to the Bishop of Cork, Bishop Lucy, to tell him that we would be coming to his diocese, but we heard nothing back from him. We bought a three-storey house on the Blackock Road, called 'Muirelinn', which means 'Our Lady With Us'. We thought that was a nice sign, as devotion to Our Lady is one of our priorities.

Having moved from Walkinstown, Kevin, Mary, their kids, and the full-time community members now lived in Cork, while the part-time community (those who held down a day job) worked and lived in our other house in Bow Lane, Dublin. It was a good setup. Kevin visited Bow Lane at least once a month to see how they were getting on. They were always delighted with a visit from Kevin and to hear what new changes were taking place.

In Cork, we went out on the street every day and talked to people about God, but it wasn't as busy as we had hoped. There wasn't the same flow of people as you'd get in Dublin. At times we were a bit lost as to what to do. We spent a lot of time in the cafés enjoying ourselves; the cakes in Cork city were amazing! We also went to see a lot of movies and even used to drive to Carrigaline, a small town nearby, whenever we had seen all the movies in the city. Before going into the Carrigaline cinema we would buy sweet coloured popcorn, cheaper in the local shop than at the cinema.

In Cork, we held a meeting once a week and invited people to it, same as we used to do in Dublin (and were now doing in Bow Lane). We had a very good response to the meeting, mostly from the people we met on the street. Quite a few Cork people would come along. Two in particular were very interested, but their families were up in arms at the thought of them becoming involved in something they knew nothing about. Several people became regulars, although it seemed that some people misunderstood us and thought we were a cult, rather than Roman Catholics just trying to spread the message of Christ.

We also tried out the Mountain Trip in Cork. We researched the whole area to see if we could find a suitable place to go on a pilgrim walk, similar to what we had in the Dublin Mountains. As we couldn't find anything really suitable, we chose to walk along the river for a couple of hours, then through the town and home again. Because the journey was so straight and there was no hill climb, we found it hard to stay awake and were falling asleep all the time. We soon abandoned that idea. One day, because of the lack of people in the city, we drove into the countryside and up into the mountains. There, we practised preaching from a mountain top. But on the drive down, the Black Van got stuck in the muck somehow and we just couldn't get it out. One of the boys had a big, heavy black coat and Kevin suggested that we put it under the wheel. So we lay the coat down in front of the wheel and revved up the engine. Lo and behold we were out of the muck! The Black Van was fine, but I'm not so sure about the black coat!

It was in Cork that Kevin got very interested in fishing, after he had paid a fishing visit to Rosscarbery, a small coastal town west of Cork city. He was amazed at the amount of fish available in the river, just up from the estuary. They were so easy to see, and it seemed they would also be easy to catch. He returned that day with a whole box of fish. We had fish for a month in the freezer!

It was then and there he decided to show us how to fish and also make the gear necessary for the job. He started out by bringing us to the local park and teaching us how to cast a line. Then, we each got a long bamboo stick, and Kevin showed us how to transform it into a fishing rod. He bought everything - the bamboo sticks, reels, whipping twine, ceramic eyes and catgut. Making the fishing rod was a painstaking process and it had to be neat. We learned to attach the reel, ceramic eyes, and the special glass top eye with whipping twine to the bamboo stick. When all the items were in place, we covered the twine areas with a type of hardening resin and left it all to dry. When the rods were made, we all made our way to the park again to test out our skills with the real thing. We spent many hours in the park every day learning how to cast. It was so much fun. The locals probably thought we were crazy. But we didn't care; it was great!

He showed us how to make lures out of feathers and fish skins (years later, in Spiddal, we would trim the beards of our goats and use the beard hair as lures for trolling). When we were good enough, which took about a week, we headed off to Rosscarbery to try out our fishing skills.

We loaded up the Black Van and off we went with our gear at around 3 o'clock in the morning. We arrived at our destination around 4am. Another thing we had learned to do was put a worm on a hook. That was a horrendous undertaking the first time, but eventually we all learned and became adept at the procedure. So there we were at 4am, freezing cold, handed our rods and worms and told to go and catch some fish.

We never really caught much fish that particular way, but Kevin discovered by chance that the area we were in had a lot of mullet. Mullet is known as a scavenger type of fish, very difficult to catch on a hook because it doesn't really take bait. Se we decided to try to 'snatch' the fish, which was also a very difficult task because the scales are thick and hard for a hook to penetrate. We waited for high water, because at that time it was easiest to spot the mullet swimming up the estuary and into the river. 'Snatching' means you cast your hook out, reel in across the fish as they are swimming past, and give the hook a good yank in the hope that the hook catches in the scales; then you try to reel in your fish. Kevin was very successful at snatching them. The first time I snatched one I was so excited! It was so heavy I couldn't haul it in myself. I had to have one of the boys help me take it in. What a feat and what a delight! It was just like nothing I had ever experienced before. We caught a huge amount of mullet between us. I think it was about four full boxes. What a catch! We brought them home, gutted them first and put them into the freezer. They tasted fabulous, especially when stuffed and baked in the oven.

We made many trips to that particular spot in Rosscarbery, always taking home a huge catch for the freezer. Everyone had their own rod. It was a real community affair and there was great excitement when someone snatched a fish. It was one thing to snatch a fish, but quite another to actually land it, especially if you snatched it in the tail. Then the fight was terrific and you usually needed someone to help you reel it in, and they'd use a hand net to lift it out of the water.

I think the mullet fishing fuelled Kevin's interest in going back to Inishere.

Kevin was always very impressed whenever he saw a catamaran. The stability of it and the safety of it as well. He thought the fact that it had two engines was very safe. So he decided to build one. He made it out of very light timber and the two crossbars were made out of very light box aluminium.

The first Catamaran

He bought an outboard motor and attached it to the centre of the back crossbar. We launched it in Kinsale harbour. It was very daring as we had no life jackets. There wasn't even a railing we could hold on to! We motored out to the mouth of the river in Kinsale. It was amazing! There were two of us standing on each pontoon and, because of our weight, the pontoon tops were nearly flush with the water. So it looked as if we were standing on the water, sliding magically along! It was scary and very exciting.

Kevin kept pushing on. He knocked down the pillars that held the gate in place at our house in Cork because he wanted to park the Black Van in the driveway. He also started to build a currach in the front garden. Martin Kennedy helped him build it and we watched it taking shape day by day. He also built a trailer for the currach. After about six months, they were ready. And then we all took a journey to Doolin, County Clare with the intention of sailing the currach out to Inishere.

Return to Inishere - 1974

The weather in Doolin was pretty windy and we didn't think we could get over to the island. But when Kevin gave the word we got into the boat and off we went, rowing out of Doolin harbour with the help of our outboard motor, on course for Inishere.

There were six of us in the currach - Kevin, Antoinette, Martin, Veronica, Vera and myself. Kevin had also designed a canvas cover for the currach, which I made. In the event that the weather got bad, the cover would prevent the boat from taking in water. As it happened, the weather was just right for the crossing, but it was raining, so the canvas cover was put over the currach with everyone sitting underneath. Everyone except Antoinette, Kevin and myself. We were at the stern. Antoinette was Kevin's assistant skipper and they sat outside the canvas, steering the outboard motor. And I sat with as little of it over me as possible, just enough to keep off the rain. It certainly was a memorable journey of about 45 minutes. I think everyone was a little afraid how things would work out, as it was all new to us. We were not what you would call 'boat people'. But seeing how confident Kevin was put us all at ease. And we had had quite a bit of practice in rowing the currach before we went to Inishere. Kevin had taken us out in Kinsale and showed us how to row. And the most important thing of all was always to keep the currach 90 degrees to the waves; otherwise a wave can catch your boat, turn it sideways and dump everyone into the water. This was something that Kevin had coached us on again and again and again. We had it imprinted on our brains what had to be done. It was mostly what can happen if there is a big swell while you're coming in to the beach. If the boat is not kept crossways to the waves, a big wave can grab the boat, turn it over in seconds, empty everyone out and everything in it and then, to top it all, smash your boat to smithereens.

When we got within about 20 feet of the island, we arose from underneath the cover and got our first vision of Inishere. Rocks and big breaking waves! Kevin gave the orders, fast and furious. We instantly got into position at the oars. Each person had their own oar. Under Kevin's direction we got the boat facing the right direction, bow to the land, and, on his word, when the right wave appeared, rowed for all we were worth. Then, at the last second, we swung the boat around so the high bow was facing the waves and the stern beached gracefully allowing the passengers to disembark. All Kevin's exhortations, warnings and advice had paid off. We were extremely happy to be on dry land. But Kevin was still shouting, while we were breaking our hearts laughing at the relief of it all working so well and glad to be ashore. He continued to give orders to draw up the currach, as there's always the danger that another big wave could catch your currach and demolish it while you're not looking.

Kevin and I made our way up to Brid and Edward's house. We got a great welcome. They had seen us coming from a long way off, recognised Kevin and were dying to hear the whole story. Every island home is equipped with a pair of binoculars, so they are able to see what's happening on the island nearest them, or when a boat is arriving or the plane taking off. Brid gave Kevin the key to the house he used to live in, we made a fire and put the kettle on the fire to make a cup of tea. Kevin's plan was to return to Doolin to bring over the rest of the gang, but decided against it as the weather was not too good. He waited until the next day to bring them over.

Kevin's Currach with cut-out section for the outboard motor.

View towards Doolin from Inishere

I can't remember much of those first few days, weeks and months, but we eventually ended up staying on Inishere. We sold the house in Cork and Mary and the kids also moved to Inishere. Now there was a huge amount of people living in a tiny house. Our sleeping quarters was a tiny room upstairs. The boys slept on one side of the room, the girls on the other. We slept in our clothes, in sleeping bags. At 1am, before we got up to say the Rosary, we would all be facing one way. Then when we went back to bed we would all face the opposite direction. We were that close, we hardly had room to sneeze. It was a lot of fun, though. We also got up at 4am to pray, then at 7am for the day.

Somehow, the news got to the local bishop that we were getting up at night-time to pray, and he suggested that we stop that. To counteract the negativity of his suggestion, Kevin suggested that we get up three times during the night. That was very hard for us. We did it for a while, but soon gave it up and resumed the two times per night.

Kevin decided to extend the house. He had lots of friends that offered advice on what exactly we should do. It was suggested that we quarry for rocks just outside our house, which was great because we didn't have to carry them too far. It was a really cool undertaking and the girls got to do the work as well. It was so satisfying to find a slab of rock and shift it out with a crowbar. The slab would just break up into pieces and the boys would carry them out and stack them for later use for building the walls of the new extension.

Kevin designed the extension, which was basically just two very large rooms. The locals were very helpful with advice and equipment. Kevin had a lot of friends on the island and they all chipped in with their advice, so there was plenty of opportunities for cups of tea and the craic.

Common room on east side

Common room interior

With the help of the islanders we constructed a scaffolding made of timber to work from. Then we made a wooden 'casing' or frame and into that we placed a layer of cement, then a layer of stones, then a layer of cement, then stones, and so on, until the rectangular wall was the height we wanted. When the walls dried, we took away the casing. Into the spaces we left in the walls went the windows and doors, and over the lot went the roof. It was very creative and we hardly noticed the cold wind that blew most of the time during the build. The extension was basically an enormous common room and a workroom beside that. The workroom was used for everything, for storage and repairs of all sorts.

Workroom on west side

Two girls from Cork joined our community, but their families were totally against them being in the community. When we moved to Inishere, the girls came with us. One of the families came out to Inishere and took one of the girls home against her will, but there was nothing we could do about it. Later, when we were working in the Claddagh, Galway fitting out the catamaran, the other girl had a visit from her family. They took her out to dinner. We never saw her again.

A big part of being in Inishere was fishing. We had a currach, but Kevin also had the timber catamaran that he built in Cork. He was always trying to make it better; removing and improving was the order of the day. To the bow, he added two cradles made out of wavin pipe for a person to stand in and fish from. It was a prime position and seemed to be very safe. One day, while we were out fishing, we came alongside a small trawler. They were giving us fish, as they had too many, and the wavin pipe caught under the gunnel of the trawler and was damaged. As soon as we got home, Kevin set about designing and building a new catamaran out of fibreglass.

Mackerel fishing was great fun in the summer time. As soon as you lowered the feathers into the water, the fish would literally throw themselves onto the hooks and, in no time at all, you had a huge amount of fish. Your dilemma was not to hit the other people in the boat with the fish dangling from your rod. You had to grab the slippery mackerel, unhook them and get the feathers out again to catch more!

The Habit

Life in Inishere was brilliant. The diversity of what we did was just terrific. It was in Inishere that we started to wear a habit. As I was a dress designer, my job was to make the habit. I hated the thought of being a nun and never wanted to be one. But, putting that aside, I just got on with the job as I didn't want to be anywhere else in the world or do anything else except be in the community. So I was stuck with whatever Kevin was inspired about!

**The habit or 'Cowl'
as it looks today.
(from the front)**

From the back

New Hairstyle

Kevin suggested one day that we all shave off our hair for God. This was a huge challenge, especially for some of the girls. It wasn't so bad for the boys as their hair was already short, but most of the girls had long hair and it looked lovely. To make a long story short, we shaved our hair off! What a challenge this was in the beginning, especially going to Mass and meeting the islanders. We only found out years later that the young men on the island were appalled at what we had done.

It didn't look too bad really.

I suppose they had designs on some of the girls, but Kevin put an end to all that. Maybe he knew, but didn't tell us the real goings on. We eventually got used to it and so did the islanders. But when you went to the mainland it was another challenge, because everyone thought you were a young boy. It was a nightmare and terribly funny, especially when we would meet up afterwards and talk about our experiences. You relied a lot on smiling rather than talking because, when you spoke, people would know you were a girl, and they might ask you, 'What's with your head shaved?' Of course, we always had strong spiritual talks so that was a terrific support for anything you would be going through.

The first habit - we called it the 'cowl' - was made out of a white woollen blanket. It was full length and had a large red cross down the front, about 3 inches wide and 4 feet long. It was a sight! The first person who volunteered to wear it was Martin Kennedy, the lad who helped Kevin build the currach in Cork. In the end, he didn't stay very long with us, but we are still great friends to this day. The cowl was a ton weight. In the beginning, it didn't have a belt or rope around the waist, so that made it extra heavy to work in. After doing a day's work, because it was white, it got really dirty. Later, we made the cowls out of white canvas. Kevin was constantly experimenting, always trying to find the perfect material for whatever we were doing, and the canvas was a bit lighter and easier to manage. But, because of being white and us always doing manual work, it also got very dirty. So we decided to dye the material navy. That was fine for a month or two, but then, with all the washing, the colour began to fade and we had a sort of denim cowl, which actually looked really cool. All in all, it was a time of immense change and great challenges.

To clean the cowls, we took them down to the lake where Kevin used to fish for eels and washed them with the use of a beetle. A beetle is a timber bat and beetle-washing was the way the islanders washed their clothes in the past, when Kevin lived on the island. The way it worked was you soaked the item of clothing in the water and then lifted it on to a flat rock. Then you beat the living daylights out of the cowl, or whatever you were washing, and that sent the dirt right through the material and, voilà, it was clean.

We had an outside toilet. The back wall of the toilet was a rock face and the sides were made of timber. A sack hung from the timber - that was the door. You threw up the sack when you entered and then let it down. Obviously, when the sack was down you would know it was occupied. But because the sack was partially transparent, you had a beautiful view of the Galway coast when using the toilet! It came a cropper when a donkey walked on top of it and fell through it. And that was the end of that toilet!

Another venture was shell-craft. We would go to many different areas on the island searching for seashells of all shapes and sizes to make ornaments with, around the lighthouse being the best place to collect them. We would take them home, wash them and make ornaments out of them, which we sold to the tourists. This was both enjoyable and successful, in that we loved creating all sorts of figures: crinoline ladies, ladies with umbrellas, frogs, etc. We loved walking out to the lighthouse because it took ages and in the spring and summer the weather was fabulous. It was a great buzz and very creative but I don't think all our ventures put together amounted to enough money to feed, clothe and house the amount of people we had in the community. Our sum total for shell craft one summer was about 500 Euro in modern money. The ornament makers thought that was wonderful. It was, of course; but not what you would call a lucrative business.

Other jobs that had to be done on a daily basis were fetching water from the well, making bread and collecting produce from the Naomh Eanna, the boat that brought all supplies to the island. It wasn't possible for such a large boat to moor at the harbour, so the currachs had to go out to the boat and collect everything that was needed. Kevin always got the girls to go out in our currach to collect the items ordered. It was always an exciting event.

We talked a lot about different ways to earn money. Even though Kevin had some money and we were mostly living off that, it wasn't going to last forever. We would have to find some means of supporting ourselves. We went fishing almost every day in the catamaran or currach. Everyone loved going fishing, especially the boys, but Kevin much preferred to take the girls out fishing. He was always afraid of the boys becoming proud if given positions of responsibility. He felt that in a mixed community a better balance of power was achieved by giving the girls most of the responsible tasks. But fishing was always a grand event. Most days we would catch plenty of fish. Because we had no way of preserving the fish or freezing it, Kevin showed us how to salt or marinate the catch. In the kitchen there was a stone bath-shaped container which was used for that purpose, but we were not always successful and lost quite a bit of fish. Eventually, Kevin decided to buy a freezer.

Kevin liked to bring up the Cat on dry land, so it wouldn't get bashed by the waves when the weather suddenly turned stormy. To be able to pull up the Cat, we made a better slipway at Pól na gCaorach beach and installed a capstan which we bought from a mainland scrapyard. With ropes, a block and tackle and everyone taking a bar, we were able to draw the Cat up onto the land.

Kevin also got the (mad) idea of setting us adrift in barrels. He would bring out the catamaran with barrels on board, throw off a barrel, then a Follower would get into the barrel with their rod and bait for fishing and Kevin would sail off to another location, leave another person in another barrel in the middle of the ocean, and come back and collect everyone later, hopefully with a barrel full of fish. Well that never really worked out, thanks be to God!

He also turned a small shed we had beside our house into a smoke house. He went to great lengths showing us how to smoke fish. We got really good at filleting the catch, colouring them in 'smoking' dye and hanging them in the smoke house to dry. When dry, each fish would be skewered and hung over the smoke fire. Kevin would set the fire going. It had to be special sawdust, set alight in a very special way: the sawdust was laid down in a spiral; the beginning of the sawdust was set alight; then it would take several hours for the fire to reach the inner end of the sawdust ring; when the fire went out, the fish were ready. They were then laid in a special timber box and sent by boat to a fish merchant in Galway.

**This was the old smokehouse, now done up
and used as a utility shed.**

Kevin also got the idea of making fish fingers. He would buy lots of packets of fish fingers, then he would take them apart and try to figure out how exactly they were made. He worked very hard on perfecting his fish fingers, which we also sold to the fish merchant in Galway. We had a nice little business going and we really enjoyed eating them as well, but unfortunately it wasn't enough to sustain us.

Kevin tried fishing with an otter board. This was a floating piece of wood with a line and baited hooks. A balloon was attached to catch the breeze and bring it out to sea. When he saw the otter board bobbing up and down, he knew there was a fish on the line and would haul it in. He loved playing around with this in his spare time, trying to make it work and he often caught fish with it.

Danish fishermen were big into clogs. The type Kevin liked had wooden soles and complete uppers made from leather or other material. He had brought a couple of pairs back from Denmark. He liked the idea of wearing clogs because the wood kept your feet warm and they were easy to mend with old car tyres. Seamus was appointed as community cobbler. If you had a shoe problem you went to him. Everyone got a new pair which we bought from IC Trawl in Howth, Co. Dublin, a Danish net-making company. They also seemed to be the fashion at the time, so we didn't look too unusual wearing them. When the rubber soles needed renewing, the car tyres made the clogs pretty heavy, but it was an economical solution. Kevin's children attended school on the island. Inishere is in a Gaeltacht area, so native Irish is the spoken language. He bought clogs for the kids, too, but they hated wearing them. Their island school pals called the clogs 'Brogaí Manaí' or 'Monk's Shoes', so on the way to school they would take them off, bury them in the sand and wear their wellingtons to school instead. They dug up their clogs on the way home and put them back on. Grown up and with their own families now, the brothers delight in relating the story! But eventually Kevin gave in and allowed them to wear regular shoes. After some years, we gave them up, too, as several people were having problems with their feet.

Because the island was full of rabbits, Kevin decided to buy a crossbow. He had previously bought a rifle, but when the police found out he had it they took it off him and said he should apply for a licence. He did apply, but never got it. One night, we went off hunting in the dark, him with his crossbow and me with a large torch. The idea of the torch was to shine the light into a field and if you saw a rabbit you would keep the beam on him and Kevin would move into position and shoot it. I don't really know how it happened, but I had to hold some part of the crossbow for Kevin while he aimed at the rabbit. I think he wasn't able to hold the crossbow steady enough, so he pulled the trigger as I was holding the crossbow and the trigger nearly blasted my thumb to kingdom come. What a pain! I was destroyed. My finger never recovered. Needless to say that was the last time I went rabbit hunting with Kevin! I can't remember if he ever caught a rabbit, but I do remember he shot a curlew. But I think there was something wrong with the curlew because it wasn't moving away when Kevin knelt down in the grass to take aim. We took it home and Mary had to cook it. It tasted like liver and was very chewy.

We often went visiting the locals at night time especially Brid and Edward, Kevin's godparents. They were so friendly and loved a visit and a chat.

The Claddagh, Galway - 1975

Building the catamaran in the Claddagh, Galway. My mother and two sisters are posing in the foreground.

As the fishing was going very well, Kevin decided to build a bigger catamaran. He designed it all on paper first, then we set about building it. The structure was made out of timber and covered with hardboard. There were two separate pontoons, which were built indoors, one at a time, in our large workroom. We covered them with many layers of fibreglass. When the pontoons were finished, we took them outside and built a deck in between them. To complete the structure was too big an enterprise for the harbour in Inishere, so Kevin decided we would finish it in the Claddagh in Galway.

There was a great send-off from Pól na gCaorach. We motored off from the land with two outboard motors and we were hardly out very far when one of the outboard motors fell off. I caught it just in the nick of time. It took us about 4 to 5 hours to sail into Galway.

We moored it as close to the slip as we could and waited for the tide to go out. Then we jacked up the catamaran on timbers so as to be able to work underneath. So began the work on the finishing of the new 'Cat'. We were again able to live in our Black Van; we had previously left it with Mary's mother, in her garden in Galway. It became our home for the next few months.

Marie, Kevin's mother, also visited to see what we were doing.

There were four of us in Galway - Kevin, Helen, Paul and myself. We had a great time while we were there. Sometimes, we would go out at night for a cup of tea to Lydons restaurant or we might go to see a movie. We worked on the Cat every day, trying to get it all together. One morning, we got chatting with a diver from Athlone. Kevin became so interested in him and the work he did, and vice versa, that we spent the whole day talking and having cups of tea. Eventually, in the evening, he invited us all out to dinner. We had a lovely time and we even looked him up later on when we were passing through Athlone, where he lived.

Life was good. It took about 6 months to complete the Cat. When it was finished, we loaded it up and took it back to Inishere. It seemed to be very heavy in the water. The weather was a little rough, and when a wave washed over the deck between the pontoons, it was fairly swamped. We had to slow down and use buckets to empty the water off it. That was quite frightening. As soon as we got to Inishere, Kevin bored holes all over the deck, so the water could escape easily.

We anchored the Cat at the Trá Mór. We made lots of fishing expeditions and Kevin's older sons often came out with us. We were fishing one day out near the 'Big Island' (Inishmore) on a beautiful sunny day, when suddenly, just off our bow, we saw the giant fin of an enormous Basking Shark. It was moving very slowly towards us, with its mouth wide open. You could have put a full-size chair in its mouth and sat on it, it was so big. We lay down at the front edge of the deck and gazed in amazement as it slid directly under us from bow to stern. It was as wide as our boat. We were so close, we could see barnacles on its skin.

Basking Shark

Bicycle Pedal Fishing Reel

Kevin installed a very unusual type of fishing reel on the Cat. It was made out of the cycling mechanism from an old bicycle. He attached eight of these reels to long fibreglass rods, four on each side of the Cat. You allowed the lures (feathers or rubber eels) to go to the sea floor and reeled up the line just off the bottom. The natural swell of the sea usually created a 'jigging' movement so the lures moved up and down to attract the fish. But you could also manually make the line 'jig' on a calm day. Then, when the fish struck, you reeled in with a hand on each pedal until the fish reached the surface and you swung in your catch. The mechanism even had gears, just like a bike!

**Pedal
Fishing Reel**

We caught lots of pollack and mackerel with this system, but it was way too much 'pedalling' work and a bit slow. Kevin later mechanised the system by installing an air compressor on board, and each reel was now an air gun instead of the bicycle pedal system. This made the line race up quickly and was much more enjoyable.

We were not back from the mainland very long when the local teenagers started to get on to the Cat at night time. When Kevin heard about that, he didn't like it and decided that maybe it was time to move on. We had been on Inishere about two years. It was sad to leave, but it was also very tough in the winter because the weather was so inclement.

Spiddal, Co. Galway 1976 - 1977

Kevin decided to look for a place on the mainland. We took the Cat to Galway, then drove in the Black Van to Spiddal. While in Spiddal, Kevin sent us around the village to see if there were any places for sale. The very first house we called on was for sale and that was the house we bought. There was a main house and several outhouses. The previous owners left behind their chickens which we looked after for a while, but then we got tired of them always coming into the house and eventually ate them all.

Mary and the family lived in the main house. We had to clean out all the sheds and outhouses for ourselves. The biggest outhouse became our common room. We laid a carpet down on the cement floor and put in the seats that Kevin had originally made for our house in Cork. We installed a cooker/burner, so our common room, at one end, was also our kitchen. And so began our stay in Spiddal.

The outhouses in Spiddal - our new home.

One of our members, Gerry Finnegan, used to sleep in the adjoining shed on his own because he would keep everyone awake with his coughing. When it snowed in the winter time, the snow would come down on top of him as he lay in his bed under a ton of blankets and heavy coats.

We had several acres of land which we tilled, and grew all our own vegetables. We collected seaweed from the sea shore, put it on the land and planted a variety of vegetables - cabbage, onions, lettuce, and more. We also grew leeks, which grew to a fantastic size, the biggest leeks I've ever seen. We got a loan of a tractor from a local farmer, made drills and popped potatoes into the drills and harvested a great crop in the summertime. It was such a different and exciting time for us, doing tasks we never in a million years dreamt we would be doing. We were now looking after animals and farming the land!

We became very interested in keeping goats. We visited a goat man in County Clare and found out all about goats. His goats were pedigree, easily manageable and beautiful to look at. We bought a huge billy goat, pure white. He was with us for awhile when we decided to get a few others. Billy and a large female went head to head for such a long time, until Billy won and became king. Then peace and quiet reigned. The smell from Billy was appalling when he was in heat, and we found it hard to drink the milk from the females, so the goats had to go! But while we had them, we were also fishing every day, and we used to cut their beards to make lures for the hooks. Brilliant lures for trolling! That's where you cast one or more lines from a boat and motor along until a chasing fish takes the lure. We originally got the goats so they would eat all the briars and grass on the land, but there was too much for them to do and they were also too much work for us.

Next on the list was cows! We had two cows, and made our own butter and also ice cream. The highlight of the week was when we made ice cream. Absolutely delicious! The cows stayed.

Another favourite homemade dessert was Kevin's 'egg flip'. It was something the Danes used to make in the war years when it was next to impossible to get chocolate or sweets. First, you get an egg and separate the white from the yolk; then beat the white for quite some time; add sugar and chocolate lumps to it. Voilà! - a fabulous, sweet treat.

Kevin enjoying his 'egg flip'

On occasion, we would go to Galway city and try to talk to people on the streets about God, but the interest was very poor, so that seemed to be a non-runner.

We did have a weekly discussion group going in Spiddal and the local priest used to come to the meetings. It was very good and informative. We also visited the local Convent of Mercy nuns and became very friendly with them.

House in Copenhagen - 1979

Kevin was friendly with an Irish girl from the Legion of Mary. Some years back, while she and Kevin were with a Legion evangelising mission to Denmark, she became friendly with a Danish man. He eventually became a Catholic and she married him and went to live in Copenhagen. They lived in an apartment attached to the Jesuit church. When Kevin sent over two people from Spiddal to do contact work in Copenhagen, they rented a room in the same apartment block and ran meetings from their own apartment. The Irish girl and her Danish husband became actively involved in the work, too. Eventually members began to come, which was a great achievement as Denmark is not Catholic. That's how Mary's Followers of the Cross started in Denmark.

Kevin never really liked Denmark very much because he felt it was the cause of a lot of young people losing their innocence. Even before we had a house there, when he had to pay an occasional visit back for business reasons, he made sure to take precautions not to be influenced by the pornography that could be seen everywhere. Before one particular visit he had a special pair of glasses made that he couldn't really see through, and he wore them all the time he was walking around Copenhagen. He didn't want to see anything by accident. Mary, his wife, had to guide him everywhere they went. Another time, he just put Vaseline on his glasses. He really went to great lengths to protect himself from the negative as he understood it. So, when we set up the new community there, he was always warning us about looking in shop windows and being careful not to see pornography. Personally, though, I never experienced anything, except how great Denmark was. But then I was brought up in Ireland, at the time a very 'sheltered' country. Kevin's upbringing may have been a whole different experience.

As they didn't have any means to support themselves or pay their rent, the members got jobs cleaning houses and working as cleaners in hotels. In their spare time, they evangelised on the streets of Copenhagen.

While two Followers were standing on the street talking to people about God, a man came along and struck one of the girls with a hatchet on the back of her neck. Then he just walked off into the crowd. Nobody really noticed what had happened, but we called the ambulance and she was rushed to hospital. Luckily, she wasn't too badly hurt, but she did have pains in her neck for a long time afterwards. Later that day, the guy turned up at our apartment. The people there had no idea he was the guy who had attacked the girl. And he was a friendly guy, so got invited in for a chat. During the conversation, he produced a huge knife, to show it off. The member he was talking with had the presence of mind and tact to casually leave the room. He called the police and they took the man into custody. My goodness!

Copenhagen was working very well, and nearly everyone learned to speak Danish fluently, which was a great achievement. It was very cold in the winter time, but the apartment was cosy, and being attached to the Jesuit church, so very easy to get Mass every morning.

It was working very well for a couple of years until the bishop called the members in for a meeting and told them they were not to wear their habit or evangelise on the street. When they continued to do this, they were called up again and told if they didn't stop there would be an announcement made from the pulpit denouncing the group. I think there may have been a policy of non-evangelisation between the Catholic Church and the Folkekirke (Church of Denmark) at the time. Maybe an ecumenical thing. We couldn't understand that, because we felt we were simply obeying the Pope's exhortation that religious communities should wear their habits, and should evangelise! Anyway, Kevin decided to pull out of Denmark. He never liked conflict, and preferred to back out when things got aggressive. This was a very hard step for all those people whom we had met and brought back to the Catholic faith. The members found it so hard that this was being taken away from them. They couldn't understand the situation at all.

Meanwhile back in Spiddal

While all this was going on in Copenhagen, we were still working away in Spiddal at various different jobs. We heard from the local fishermen that there was a demand for periwinkles. Kevin sent us off with buckets to pick them. It was great fun. We had a super time collecting them among the rocks on the seashore. The best spots were on the sheltered side of the rock, where all the winkles would gather together away from the waves and wind. If you found a good place, you could nearly fill up your entire bucket, which was quite a large-size bucket. Typically, a couple of hours would fill it. I think the going price at that time was £20 per cwt. The girls were very good at it, but the boys hated it! One of them said that, after a day's picking, when he went to bed at night, all he saw in his sleep all night was millions of periwinkles! It was great work, but your fingers were worn out in no time. Then we took to wearing rubber gloves, which were not as nimble or effective. It wasn't very long, however, before we cleaned out the whole area of periwinkles.

Periwinkle

Clam Digging

Another vibe that came in through the local fishermen was an urgent request for people to dig clams. The place to do that was in Clarinbridge, County Galway, a place famous for the mollusks. We got all the tools together - spades, forks, buckets, wellingtons, rain gear and a small rowing boat to take us out to the clam banks. We drove off in our Black Van and set up home for the next few days in Clarinbridge. When we arrived, there were already groups of diggers out on the banks working away. We were eager to get started.

Kevin took the first crew out at about 5am in the morning, when it was still dark. He would stop the boat over the clam banks, as the tide was high at this stage, then you were told to hop out of the boat. It felt like you were jumping out into very deep water, the water sometimes being practically up to your waist. You were both terrified and very excited to get started. It wasn't really dangerous as the tide was on the way out and once it started to go out it went out very fast. As the tide receded, you found yourself on the bank, digging right away, as it wouldn't be long before the tide would start to come in again. You dug down with your fork, lifted up as much as you could, turned it over on the dry seabed and sorted out the full from the empty clams; and they were plentiful, the empty ones. You put the good clams into buckets. Louis, Kevin's son, who was only about 12 years old at the time, loved anything to do with boats. He got the job of collecting our clams (we emptied our buckets into his little boat) and keeping us well fed by delivering our food and also ferrying people back and over when someone wanted a break. It all had to be timed very well, especially when the tide was on the turn. A watchful eye had to be kept on the last diggers to make sure they were all taken back to land before it got dark or the tide got too high. Otherwise they would have to swim ashore! Kevin would be out in the little boat for a last look around to make sure no one was left behind. It could get quite dark and, with no lights to show up who was left, you had to shout to let him know where you were. Thank God, all heads were counted and everyone had a terrific meal and a super night's sleep when the day was over.

The clam digging lasted about a week. Midweek, Kevin decided to return to Spiddal to bring back the catamaran. Because it had such a shallow draft, it was able to manoeuvre in very low water, which was perfect for gathering the clams from the diggers, also saving a lot of toing and froing in the little boat. That week, we hadn't much time for anything else except dig, eat, sleep. We were up each morning at 5 or 6am. Some of the boys found the work very hard.

The Longline System

While in Spiddal, Kevin got very interested in longline fishing, especially after he heard about a Norwegian automatic system. He remembered that was the way the Faroese used to fish - a long rope, with baited hooks attached by short pieces of string (snoods) about a metre apart. But the Faroese baited each hook by hand, which was slow and tedious. This Norwegian system was all automated. The beauty of longlining, as opposed to net fishing, is that you only catch big fish, the small ones being left to grow. So it is much more environmentally friendly and sustainable. He was very impressed with this system especially because of the speed of the automatic baiting system.

He was so interested in the system that we took a trip to Ålesund on the west coast of Norway to see it working on a boat there. It was amazing, and Kevin was absolutely fascinated by it. When we got home again, Kevin continued to work on the system he was developing and, with his new-found inspiration, he was full of enthusiasm.

Kevin installed his first longline system on the Cat. We would go out fishing, test the system to see how it performed, then if there was any flaw at all, we would return to base and start working on perfecting that. So, new and exciting developments were happening all the time. He continued to develop and perfect his Bait Hopper, Baiting Box, Magazine for holding line and hooks and, of course, the Splitter. The Splitter was the most important piece of equipment. It automated putting the hooks up onto the Magazine rail while the longline was being hauled in from the sea. Otherwise, as I said, you'd have to do that by hand which, traditionally, was slow and messy with tangles and hooks getting stuck in your hand.

Early Development of the Longline System on the Catamaran

 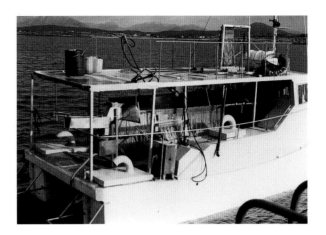

Later Development of the Longline System on the Catamaran

We even bought a 'Fastworker' to develop the system for small boats.

Speaking of 'hooks in hand' - when 'shooting' the longline into the sea, the hooks were guided from the Magazine rail in through the Baiting Box, where each hook would pick up a piece of bait and go out into the sea and start fishing as soon as the line reached the sea bed. It happened that once, during an experiment, when the line was flying out at top speed, Seamus, who was feeding the Bait Hopper with bait, got a hook in his thumb. There was a great commotion, shouting and screaming and putting the Cat into reverse so we could help him get the hook out of his thumb. Kevin got a pliers, cut the hook, and took it out. We continued shooting of the line when, lo and behold, it happened again! This time, a hook caught in his little finger! After that episode we had to go back to the drawing board and correct the flaw as we couldn't have that happening! Seamus always tells a funny story about that event, which was horrendous really. Anyway, thumb and little finger recovered completely!

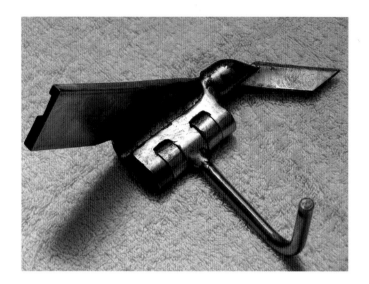

Splitter

Magazine
and
Baiting
Box

Although the system was working successfully on the Cat, Kevin thought if he was going to interest the ordinary fisherman who was used to trawling, he would need a conventional boat to put it on. So we set off for England to see if we could buy a second-hand trawler. We did a tour of the west coast of England, eventually settling in the beautiful town of Whitby where we discovered a boat for sale called the Whitby Light, a 50 ft trawler in pretty good condition.

Our stay in Whitby was wonderful. The people were extremely friendly, amazingly friendly! They treated us like kings, inviting us for dinner, allowing us to use their bathroom and shower facilities, giving us food. There was no end to their hospitality. One day, as they were working on the pier, Kevin happened to walk across their nets to cross the road. As he passed over the nets, they shouted, 'We've caught a monkfish!' We all had a great laugh. When we eventually bought the boat, we had to undertake the sailing of it back to Ireland.

Kevin sent for the crew back in Spiddal. Paul and Seamus made the journey over and we took the boat back via the Caledonian Canal. What a trip! It was terrific except for the time we went aground. We were heading down the canal and saw a bridge and thought that must be the way. Suddenly we hit bottom. But it wasn't a problem. Kevin just waited until the boat swung around and we were on our way again, this time in the right direction. One area that has stuck in my mind is a place called 'The Great Race', in the southern Outer Hebrides. We were stuck in the same spot for about an hour. The current was so strong we just hadn't the power to outwit it. Then we decided to just go with the current, which worked out fine. We were on our way again!

Our route took us north from Whitby to the Caledonian Canal, through the Canal, down through the Hebrides and across to Lough Swilly in Northern Ireland. Then west and around Donegal to Galway. The harbour in Spiddal wasn't very safe for such a big boat, so Kevin docked it in Galway harbour.

For the next few weeks, we drove in from Spiddal to the Whitby Light and, under the direction of Kevin, the boat was stripped down to see what needed repairing. Both boys and girls have great memories of cleaning out the bilges, then setting about painting them white. Kevin liked a very tidy and spotlessly clean ship, with the bilges painted white, making it easy to see if there was a leak, which could be attended to right away. The deck was tarred so no water could seep through into the sleeping quarters. We kitted out the boat for the longline system, at the same time as giving it a complete revamp.

Whitby Light through the years with
Longline and 'Jigging' systems onboard.

The Quest

Be selfish for unselfish reasons
and unselfish for selfish reasons.

Kevin Jacobsen

While in Spiddal, we undertook what we called the 'Quest'. The Quest was based on the Gospel message where Christ sent out the Apostles two by two to preach the Gospel. Not to take anything with them, no purse, etc. We were sent out in threes - two girls and a boy. The only possession we had with us, besides our habit and cloak, was a raincoat. The raincoat, which I had to make for everyone, was yellow and made from very strong, durable, waterproof material. It had inside pockets right around the whole coat. You could carry a few essentials, like your passport, etc., in the pockets. We started off from Spiddal by hitching to Dublin. Once we got to Dublin we then headed out to different areas in Dublin to beg for the money to get to Denmark, which is where we were all headed.

**Visiting my family home before the Quest.
Left to right:
Me, my Dad, Maureen, my Mam, Michael (at the back), Mena (front) and Kevin**

Kevin, Maura and I went to Ballyfermot. Even though we were scared that we wouldn't get very far, we still went ahead. The reception we got in Ballyfermot was just amazing. The people were so friendly and open. They invited us into their homes, made us sandwiches and tea and were really interested in what we were about to undertake. At one house the owner gave us a packet of teacake mixture. She said that was all she had, so we took it. At another house a woman gave us a sponge (the type you clean off your table with). It was so funny, but we were delighted to get anything. Eventually we had enough money between us to get the ferry from Dun Laoghaire to Holyhead. We were giddy we were so delighted. After hitching from Holyhead to Dover, we were again delighted to meet some of the others from the community who made it to there as well.

We were so hungry when we got there that Kevin took out the teacake mixture and mixed some water with the powder and then gave it out in the little fancy paper cups that come with it to anyone who wanted it. I think we all had some we were so hungry. We then slept underneath the stairs in the ferry ticket hall in Dover. When we woke up in the morning all we could see were feet all around us belonging to the people queueing up to get their tickets.

Eventually we boarded the boat. Because we were still hungry, Kevin sent one of the girls, Anne Doyle, into the kitchen to ask if they had any leftover scraps they could give us. Anne returned with a tray full of food and drink. We laughed our heads off we were so happy. The food was just wonderful! When we got to Belgium we waved goodbye to our community friends and started off hitching again. We had to go through Belgium, then Germany and into Denmark. A lovely gentleman who had just left his son to school picked us up in Belgium and brought us to a restaurant for a meal. Heaven sent! He said the reason he picked us up was because he was lonely after leaving off his son. Another guy picked us up in Belgium and brought us home to stay the night in his apartment, which was tiny. He gave us a place on the floor on each side of his bed. Then hopped into the bed himself and started smoking! We could hardly stop laughing, it was such a funny situation. In the morning, he got up, dressed himself and left immediately. We had no idea where he went. We didn't speak French and he didn't speak English. He returned about 20 minutes later with fresh French bread, cakes and lots of goodies. We had a wonderful breakfast and then he brought us to the spot where we could start hitching again.

We were then picked up by a German family who had been to Disneyland in France. The wife was a nurse. When we got to their house, they said we could have a bath or shower while they made dinner. They allowed us to sleep on the floor in their sitting room.

They were just some of the highlights of our questing to Denmark. It took us about 11 days to get there altogether and we nearly all arrived within a few days of each other. We did the quest several times, both around Ireland and around Denmark.

One of the times that we went to Denmark, Kevin, instead of questing back to Ireland, decided he would take the ferry boat to the Faroe Islands from Copenhagen. The Faroe Islands are between the Shetland Islands and Iceland. He wanted to pay a visit to his relations and to find out all he could about the longline system of fishing up there. It was a very exciting trip for the three of us - Kevin, Maura and myself. We loved every minute of it. When we got home to Spiddal Kevin continued to work on the system, perfecting it all the time, until he felt it was ready for demonstration.

Me examining Faroese Longlines

Kevin on board a Faroese boat

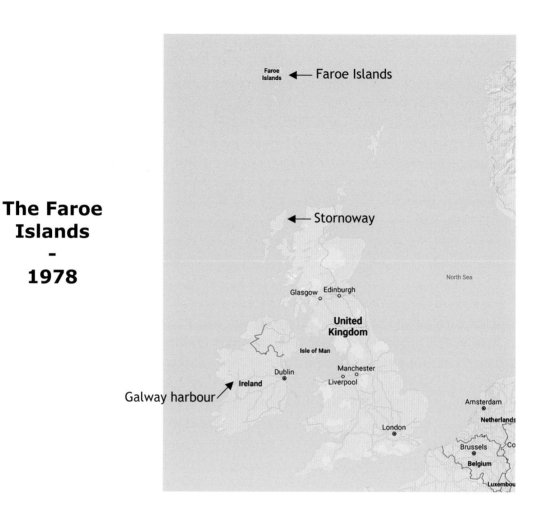

**The Faroe
Islands
-
1978**

Where there is grace, there is new

discovery... adventure.

Kevin Jacobsen

When Kevin felt the longline system was ready for demonstration, he wanted to take it to the Faroe Islands. We left Galway harbour one beautiful summer's day, the first leg of the journey to the Faroes. Kevin had been watching the weather forecast for quite some time, checking constantly to see when would be the best time to make our move. We steamed up to Stornoway in Scotland and stayed there for the night. The weather was absolutely perfect. Dead calm. All was going as planned. The next day we continued on our way. The sea was quite choppy, not as nice as the previous day, but we had our Decca Navigaor. What a brilliant machine, terrific for keeping us on course.

It took us another day to reach the Faroe Islands. It was amazing to actually hit them right on target, 5 or 6 tiny islands in the middle of nowhere. All the girls were sick on the journey there. We just lay in a comfortable position wherever we could find a space and stayed in that position until we arrived in Torshavn.

The islands were an amazing sight. To sail into Torshavn, the capital, was just fabulous. All the houses were brightly painted and they also had grass on their roofs which looked fantastic. Although I had seen Torshavn before on the previous trip, it was beautiful to see from the Whitby Light. As we arrived and headed towards the pier, Kevin gave the command to Paul to tie up at the nearest bollard, at the bow. So Paul ran up to the bow and jumped off onto the pier, threw the rope over the bollard and jumped back onto the boat, which he missed and landed on the rope! He went down with the rope and then, as the boat moved away, Paul's head appeared at the top of the bow. When he was level with the deck he just hopped on board, not a bother on him. We got a great welcome from the people, and a round of applause for Paul's amusing stunt.

Kevin had relations there. His cousin, Egil Restoff, owned a bakers shop, and we used to buy our bread from him every day. He also had a relation who owned a hotel and who invited us all for dinner. We enjoyed it immensely, eating everything that was put before us. We were always starving. Kevin was embarrassed, I think.

Fishing in the Faroe Islands was a delight. There were fish in abundance. We didn't have to go out very far at all to catch them. They were so plentiful and really very big. The normal whiting in Ireland would be about 20cm long, but up there the whiting were as big as salmon. They also had a lot of species, such as 'brosme', that we didn't have in Irish waters, that also tasted delicious. The longline system worked fantastic and the locals were very impressed with it, but not at all interested in buying it. We stayed for about a month. In that time we also worked on the street, talking to the people about God, trying to interest them in loving God. We found the young people were not that interested. What they seemed to enjoy a lot was motoring around in their cars.

It was a brilliant experience. We steamed around most of the Faroe Islands, getting a great impression of the fishing capabilities and breathing in the spectacular scenery.

Torshavn

Howth Road - 1979

On our journey back from the Faroes, instead of returning to Galway, Kevin felt inspired by the Holy Spirit to sail on around to Dublin. We pulled into Howth Harbour and bought a house on Howth Road. We already had the house in Bow Lane, so he decided to sell that. When the house was ready in Howth Road, Mary and the children came up to live. Kevin's eldest son, Louis, stayed in Galway, as he was studying to be a tool maker. In Howth Road we began to set up all the machinery needed to manufacture the longline system. When it was all installed, Louis came up to Dublin and showed us how to use the machines, especially the lathe and milling machines.

One day, Kevin wanted to buy some pipe for the longline system. He went to the scrapyard and pulled out the pipes he wanted. On taking them home we found they were full of chocolate! Our next problem was how to get the chocolate out of the pipes so we could eat it. The pipes came from Cadbury's. They were changing their pipes to stainless steel and so were ditching the old ones. Michael cut the pipes into foot-length pieces and heated each one over the gas ring. Voila! The chocolate slid out in one piece. We had bags and bags of chocolate, which we offered to our relations and friends and kept some for our egg flip in the evening.

We continued to fish out of Howth, testing the longline system all the time. Howth was not a great place to fish. The waters were very dirty with all sorts of garbage and strange things coming up on the lines. We thought that could be because of Sellafield.

We exhibited the system in the RDS in Dublin at a technical show and it won an award for Best Innovative Design. We also took it to Copenhagen, Denmark and exhibited in the Bella Centre. Kevin continued to perfect the longline system, while we went out on the street talking to the youth about loving God and having our weekly meetings.

Longline System 'Hauling' Side of unit

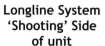

Longline System 'Shooting' Side of unit

Roundstone, Co. Galway 1980 - 1990

The Danish family who had been with us in Copenhagen came and joined us in Howth Road when we closed the house in Denmark. As our community expanded, Kevin decided to look for a bigger place in the country that would be more suited to community expansion and living.

He went scouting in the west of Ireland and eventually settled on a house in Roundstone, fifty miles west of Galway City. It was a two-storey house on 35 acres of land. The house was previously used as a holiday home. It wasn't really well cared for that much and was in great need of repair. Kevin sent a team ahead to work on it and turn it into a liveable condition. One of the first jobs to be tackled was the building of the sceptic tank. We built it big enough for 40 people. It was as big as a house. There was also an overgrown garden, sheltered by a high wall, perfect for growing vegetables - a real sun-trap. We tilled the garden and grew our own vegetables. We had a fabulous common room on the upper floor looking out onto the sea. The land bordered a beautiful beach, fabulous in the summer time.

After we all eventually moved and were settled, the community grew to include four families altogether. Two of the families lived in separate mobile homes on the land. The other two families lived in the community house.

Our house in
Roundstone

We moved there in 1980 and worked hard to improve the whole enclave. We were never short of work to be done. One of the first things we did when we came to Roundstone was to improve the roads on the land. Kevin wanted the roads to be completely covered with sand and also to make them so good that we could drive on them as well as walk on them. The boys did all that work, but the girls were able to help out as well - driving the dumper which carried rocks and operating the JCB for lifting the rocks onto the dumper.

Another project was to revamp the harbour. Originally, when the tide went out, the whole harbour bed was covered with stones. Kevin wanted all the stones removed so that when the boat was resting on the bottom no stone would go up through the hull and make a hole. We completely revamped the whole harbour, built a slipway and did up a place for mooring our Cat. We also brought the Whitby Light into the very small harbour, but it wasn't safe enough for a 50ft trawler so we moored it outside the main harbour in Roundstone town. Our house was only a mile from the town.

Kevin wanted some way of keeping the grass trimmed. He was always talking about how sheep did a great job of eating grass so it never grew very long. He thought of investing in a couple of sheep. We bought a few from a local farmer, but spent our time running after them when they wandered off onto our neighbour's land. And they were extremely hard to catch without a sheepdog, which we didn't have. We had plenty of land for them to keep trimmed but, unfortunately, we couldn't really control them. We had to spend too much time going off looking for them, bringing them back, trying to block up all the ways they would get out. It was an endless job! We eventually had to let them go. But not before the cutest one made a cameo appearance in one of our home movies; it was hilarious trying to get it to 'act' the way we wanted.

Then we invested in a couple of cows. One of them was a Jersey cow, a beautiful looking animal. We named her 'Edwina'! The milk from her was fantastic. It made delicious ice cream!

We needed a generator for electricity to keep our business going because the electricity in the area was always going down. We built a house for the generator, and set up a workshop and work areas in all the outhouses. Then we began the manufacturing of the longline system. In the beginning we bought braided line for the system, but because the line didn't work too well, Kevin decided we would buy braiding machines and make the line ourselves. He sent Seamus to England to learn about braiding machines and to purchase the right ones, which he did. He set up the braiding machines in one of the outhouses and started to make the line. As we began to manufacture the longline system, we needed more space. We eventually got a grant to build a workshop. We still had the Whitby Light, which was used extensively for experimental work for the longline system and also to show clients when they came to see the system in operation.

Some of the places where our system was installed...

Iceland 1981

Denmark 1982

France 1982

Algeria 1983

Norway 1983

Although the longline system worked very well for us and we sold it to several fisherman in Denmark, England, France and Iceland, it never really took off as a commercial venture. However, a man came visiting us from Northern Ireland and, when he saw our braiding machinery, suggested to Kevin and Seamus that we should set up a braided cord business. He gave us samples of nylon and polyester yarn, and practically showed us how to do everything. We eventually set up the machines to make the line and then got customers in the fishing, twine, cord and venetian blind businesses that bought our line on an ongoing basis. We called our line 'Speedoline'.

Our braiding factory

74

Our land in Roundstone was overrun with rabbits. They were eating up not just our land but all the surrounding commonage. After much thought, rifles were bought. It was a great experience to go rabbit hunting with Bernard and Kevin. You were given a haversack and each rabbit shot would be put into the bag. As the night wore on you ended up with a haversack of hot rabbits. It was weird and wonderful. But it was always lovely to be out in nature and to see so many rabbits hopping about. They were really very plentiful. Veronica became an expert at skinning rabbits and making all sorts of delicious dishes, especially rabbit stew.

Families leave the community

As some of the children who belonged to the families in the community became teenagers, they seemed to become ashamed of their parents being community members. They didn't want to be seen with them. This is fairly common with teenagers, anyway, as they have to find their own way in life. It wasn't long before all the families left.

Start of Movie making

Besides fishing, filming was becoming a passion for Kevin. He loved the idea of creating a beautiful film with high ideals, set in fabulous locations all around Ireland. The idea had germinated while making promotional videos of the longline system. He saw advertised a filming course in RTE, so he decided that he and I would both do the course. We signed up and, on the very first day, Kevin got very restless, wandered off from the course and on to the set of a TV series that they were making with Anna Manahan. He spent the entire duration of the course on the set. They welcomed him and he became part of the whole thing. They were so impressed with his interest in everything that was taking place that they allowed him to come every day. He thoroughly enjoyed every minute of it. And, of course, he learned loads.

The Servants of Love

It was in Roundstone that we changed our community name to the Servants of Love. The world, and we, had changed since our Legion days and needed a more positive approach to spirituality. The emphasis now was more on love, friendship, compassion and solidarity.

We started filming and bought a small caravan which we used as our base while on location in remote areas of Connemara. Seamus was getting more and more into composing his own music, and I was making meditation programmes on cassette tape. But living way out in the West of Ireland in the late 1980s, we were cut off from the rest of the world.

We discussed this and concluded that to effectively share our Christian message and high ideals would mean moving from Roundstone.

Wicklow - 1990

When Kevin decided that we were going to leave Roundstone, Co. Galway, he took a trip to Dublin with Maura, a member of the community. The idea was to try to find a place as near as possible to Dublin, since the hub of the film industry business was centred there and because we were trying to learn everything we could about the business. They went looking along the east coast, north and south of Dublin, eventually settling in Wicklow Town.

When Kevin returned from his trip, he told us he had found a fabulous place by the sea that was surrounded by parks and had a beautiful harbour to moor our boat. There was just no end to the talents that Wicklow had! If we moved there we would be practically in the town, near the church, shops, mountain walks and, of course, the sea for swimming in the summer time. There were so many advantages to moving to Wicklow.

His plan was that we were going to try to be in the new premises before Christmas 1990. Kevin decided that four would go ahead of the pack - Seamus, Gay, Maura and himself. We packed up our belongings, hitched the caravan onto our van and off we went to Wicklow. When we arrived at the premises, I was appalled at the state of the place! Two huge gates covered with barbed wire, the house that we were moving into was not a house at all, but two warehouses that were extremely dirty. No kitchen, no nothing. When we told the people who were selling the premises to us that we were going to move in, they were incredulous and wouldn't allow us to do that until all the papers were signed and sealed. We never saw the hand of God so clearly in that undertaking. We were all thrilled, except Kevin. He got very down at the thought of not getting into the house. We were delighted to be able to go home to Galway and let the others know exactly what the place was like. It also gave us a little respite before the eventual move which was in another 3 weeks time. I was so happy.

We were much more prepared the second time round. Once we were in and it was ours we were more resigned and positive about the whole move. We started the clean-up. We moved our caravan into the warehouse and worked from there. We eventually discovered a kitchen, which had been used as a canteen when the place was a fish factory. Terrific! We put up our TV in the kitchen, went Christmas shopping and had a lovely Christmas, just the four of us in Wicklow 1990. Eventually the rest of the community joined us in January.

Fishing with Bow and Arrow

After we gave up the longline system and Kevin became more interested in filming, he also took up fishing as a hobby. He had seen several very big mullet in Wicklow harbour and became fascinated with them. We had a very small boat, for which he made a cute little fibreglass seat and strengthened the stern to attach an outboard motor. He also installed a place in the little boat for storing the fish he would catch. He used to launch the boat in the harbour and steam up the river to the Broadlough, a shallow, salt water lake about a kilometre inland. As you can't really catch mullet on a rod, except by snatching them, he decided to use his old crossbow. But the police found out about it and confiscated it!

After the police took his crossbow, Kevin immediately explored his next option. A bow and arrow. He set up a bale of hay in our film studio with a bull's eye on it and practised every day to see if he could hit the target. He practised relentlessly, never letting up or thinking that he couldn't do it. Eventually, when he felt he was proficient enough, he starting getting all the gear together to go fishing. He attached a fishing reel to the bow and monofilament to the arrow, sharpened the arrow end so that it would penetrate the hard scales of the fish and, together with his polaroid glasses, sun hat and fishing outfit, off he went. He had it down to a fine art. He would nearly always return home with 4 or 5 really big fish. He loved it. In the beginning, he kept missing the fish when he would shoot the arrow, but eventually he became so good at it that he always returned with a box of fish. I enjoyed going along on the fishing trip with Kevin. If you went by car to the spot, you had to walk through reeds that were higher than your head, which was an eerie experience. This would go on for about ten minutes till you got to the spot. Then Kevin would unpack his gear, along with his polaroid attachments. He wore glasses anyway, so he would flip the polaroids up and down as the case may be and then start shooting the fish as they came closer to the bank. No sound was to be made, otherwise the fish would be frightened off. It worked like a treat.

Mark, Kevin's son, enjoying Kevin's modified Bow and Arrow.

Paul also had his kit and occasionally joined in the 'fishing'.

Not everything is in the photos, but Kevin added shoulder support, barbed arrow heads, fishing reel and other gadgets to make the system effective.
The bows were also 'geared' so when you pulled back the string, you could relax as you took aim because the bow 'held' the arrow in place until you let it go.

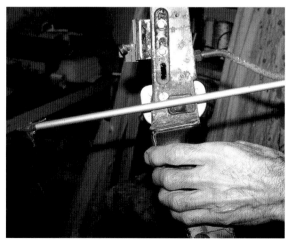

Kevin's Healing Journey

About a year before we moved to Wicklow, Margaret, one of our members, found Kevin on the floor in his room writhing in pain, unable to move. He went to the doctor and found out he had angina. Angina is a symptom of coronary heart disease. It's basically chest pain caused by reduced blood flow to the heart. The doctor gave him a prescription for pills. When we bought the pills at a chemist in Galway, Maura and I were amazed at the price! We discussed what we could we do about the cost. Surely there was another solution.

When we eventually moved to Wicklow, Nuala was in the library one day and found a book called 'Fit for Life' by Marilyn and Harvey Diamond. It was life-changing. After reading the book we couldn't wait to change our diet. Harvey Diamond's father had died of a heart attack, and he didn't want to end up the same way. So he invented a diet where you ate only fruit until 12 noon, thereby losing weight. The book caused a health revolution in America and in our community as well. Kevin embraced the new diet, only fruit until 12 noon. He quickly lost weight and had lots of energy.

Wheatgrass Juice

He discovered Wheatgrass Juice when he paid a visit to the Dublin Food Co-op. There, he met Bernadette Bohan who had twice cured herself of cancer. She told him all about wheatgrass and how easy it was to grow. After he had an in-depth chat with her about the benefits of it, he was hooked. He bought the seeds and started the process of soaking them and growing and drinking wheatgrass juice. He also loved putting it on his skin. He would spread it all over his head and off he would go to Mass in the morning with a green head. He didn't care what others thought of him. He just believed so much in the healing properties of it. He eventually got his health back through fruit in the morning, wheatgrass and generally changing his diet.

The idea behind the fruit until 12 noon was that eating raw food until midday gives your body a chance to rid itself of waste products accumulated from the previous day. This would also supply your body with plenty of energy. Raw food has its own enzymes and so is easily digested. But when you eat cooked food, the enzymes are killed by the high cooking temperature, so your body then draws on its own enzymes which are there for healing. The lack of raw food and a surplus of cooked food means your body becomes depleted of its enzymes and this gets worse until you eventually get sick.

But raw food gives your digestion a break from having to supply enzymes all the time. Hence all the energy you have while on the raw food diet. This was a great revelation to Kevin and the rest of the community. And it was a great way to lose weight!

We all eventually moved over to the raw diet. Kevin was very enthusiastic about that too, so enthusiastic that he decided he wanted to open a raw food restaurant. But before he did that he thought it might be a good idea to visit the best raw restaurants in the States because the USA seemed to be where they all were. Kevin wanted to learn how to create appetising healthy dishes.

Working in US Raw Food Kitchens

He headed off with Veronica, our chef, to Los Angeles. They visited a friend of mine called Beverly who brought them to visit Juliano's, a raw food restaurant in Santa Monica. As
they pulled up outside his place, they caught sight of Juliano about to leave his premises. Beverly encouraged them to go speak with him directly and ask if they could work for him. They made a dash to talk to him. He hesitated a little but then agreed to take them on for free. They were delighted. Juliano's usual consultancy fee was $1,000 an hour! They worked for him for about a month and acquired invaluable experience and information.

They moved on to San Francisco, where they had a funny experience. One day, as they were walking along the road, they were accosted by a down-and-out who tried to rob their sleeping bags. But a whole crowd of down-and-outs came to their rescue!

They visited Roxanne's in San Francisco. Her place was amazing. Her dishes were astounding, so they took plenty of notes.

Then they went to Las Vegas where they met a lovely chef who was more than helpful and generous because he shared some raw food recipes with them.

Back in Los Angeles, they met a raw food chef called Ito, who was Korean. He had taken a vow of silence and hadn't spoken for several years. He hired them. They got on great with him despite the fact that he never spoke a word. He brought them home to his house and they stayed with him for a while, learning all the time from his raw creations. When he saw the state of their sleeping bags, it was a wonder the down-and-out actually tried to rob them. Ito bought them new ones!

Then they found other raw food restaurants that took them on. They made their way around the States, ending up in New York where they trekked from raw food restaurant to raw food restaurant, tasting and taking notes on everything, and photos as well.

Juliano

Roxanne's
website

Veronica with
Ito

Raw Food comes to Ireland

When Kevin returned home he couldn't wait to try out all he had learned. He spent all his waking moments working on the new recipes. Every day he would make something different and then try it out on us to see if we liked it. The first thing he created was the Vegan Wrap. It was the friendly chef in Las Vegas who had shared with him how to make them so that he could recreate them when he was back in Ireland.

When Kevin eventually got them right, he then wanted to produce them on a large scale. So he invented a huge Dehydrator for the purpose.

**Kevin's Dehydrator
- the large white
object.**

Kevin's Vegan Wrap

He designed the whole thing himself and we used it for four and a half years. It was brilliant. The only drawback was that our wrap chef, Paul, had to get up in the middle of the night to turn the cradles that held the wraps. So, after four and a half years, we decided to invest in regular dehydrators to see if they would work. Well, we've been using them ever since, but we haven't been quite able to reach the same output that Kevin reached with his dehydrator. He wasn't really finished with modifying the machine when he died and he didn't have anything written down about it. So, for a while, wrap-making was a little hit and miss. But I think Paul has finally mastered the art of making the perfect wrap.

Carrageen Cake and Coconut Cream
The next thing Kevin concentrated on was making a healthy Carrageen Cake. He made thousands of experiments until he came up with the perfect recipe. Then he started on his Coconut Cream. He just went from one thing to the next, trying to create the perfect raw food dessert, wrap or whatever would enhance the diet of a person transitioning from ordinary cooked food to a raw food diet. He wanted to make it easy for people to make the change.

Optimum Health Programme
He made out a programme, Optimum Health, whereby he would introduce people to a healthy diet. His intention was to contact all the religious houses and talk to them about trying to incorporate raw food into their regime. He sent out a lot of flyers and waited to see if he would get a response. He got some interested replies from a few places and was booked to give a talk and a demonstration. On the run-up to the demo day he became quite sick. It seemed to be a problem with his back. He couldn't lie down and he couldn't stand without having to lean over something. In fact, to sleep he had to stand and lie forward over a table and try to get some

rest that way. His condition improved so that he could lie down, but still not stand, and as the day approached for his talk, it seemed very unlikely that he would be able to do it. But there was no stopping Kevin!

He had to be driven to the location, prone, in our camper van. On his arrival, he got out on crutches and made his way to the room to give the talk. Everyone was very impressed with his talk and they became really interested, and then at lunch time he had to go back out to the camper and lie down again. Then back again after lunch to give the rest of the talk. When the talk was over, he hobbled out to the camper again, lay down and was driven home. It was so funny really, you had to laugh. Here was a man talking about changing your diet and he couldn't even walk into the place to give the talk. But Kevin was extraordinary. He had no thought for himself. He was only concerned that they had hired him and no matter what condition he was in he was going to give his talk.

Frozen Shoulder

Kevin suffered a lot of pain in his time on earth. Not excruciatingly bad pain, but pain nevertheless. He had a type of pain in his shoulder called 'frozen shoulder'. I believe he got it from excessively hard work when he was young, on the boats. He loved to put heat on it. We invested in quite a few heat pads and during the winter he would wear a heat pad on his shoulder all the time. He had it rigged up so he could leave the heat pad on his shoulder and just unplug it when he was moving around; and then just plug it in again wherever he would sit or lie down. He had electrical connectors all over the house for this purpose, including at the community table where we gathered for meals.

To write his movie scripts and get some heat in the winter, he travelled to the Canary Islands and also to Marbella, Spain. While in the Canaries, he hired a car and bought a little blanket, and slept in the car with just the little blanket. He used to enjoy seeing all the people sitting outside their houses, and he also loved walking down to the little harbours and doing some fishing. When he was in Mogan, a harbour on the island of Gran Canaria, he spotted a lot of mullet among the fancy yachts. Off he went to buy some fishing gear and proceeded to catch loads

Kevin in Mogan, still after the mullet

of them. He fried them at the side of the road and had a feast. He was told several times that it wasn't allowed, but that didn't stop Kevin. He just returned to a different spot and continued fishing!

The Movie Business

One of the reasons we had moved to Wicklow from Roundstone, Co. Galway in 1990 was to be closer to the filming community. In Roundstone, Kevin had become very interested in making films through the longline system. He wanted to film the system in order to market it, so he purchased a video camera and made a corporate video of the longline system. But then he got really interested in making films with a deeper meaning. He thought it would be great to spread the message of true love. So he set about writing scripts and getting the community members to act in them.

He became director and script writer; Paul and I became camera persons; Seamus became the composer and the rest of the community became actors, or whatever was needed on any given filming day.

It was a time of great upheaval within the community. Previous to that time, the girls all had their heads shaved and wore veils. So now acting required that we wear a wig! At first we just bought cheap wigs that you could buy in a toy shop. They were ridiculously funny! Later on, thankfully, friends and family donated old wigs they had no use for anymore. We had great fun with them. But finally it turned out that growing our hair was the cheapest and most credible option.

Kevin directing, with Paul on camera.

In Roundstone and later, Wicklow, we made several films, all written by Kevin. He would do all the post production work himself, then show them to the community to see how they could be improved.

More Inventions

Of course, he made all his own equipment in the workshop. One of the first things he did was try to improve the speed of filming two people in conversation by making a movable camera stand.

The stand was a contraption made from an old bicycle, well mainly just the wheel. The camera was mounted on the wheel which was attached to an arm that moved on a bearing connected to the ceiling in the centre of the room. The actors would be seated in the centre of the room facing each other. All the camera person had to do was wheel the camera around to face each actor, making it very easy and quick to get the opposite point of view. This also made the film much easier to edit as it was all shot in sequence. Line by line.

Kevin was also very impressed by Steadicam - this was a 'steadying' apparatus strapped to the camera person's body on which the camera was mounted. It enabled the camera person to record non-shaky pictures while moving with the actors who might be walking, running etc. Shooting in this continuous manner also reduced editing afterwards. Kevin sent Bernard, a member of the community, to a supplier in England to have a look at the Steadicam. They demonstrated to him how it worked. The cost of £25,000, however, was prohibitive. So Kevin decided to make his own. Between what Bernard could remember and Kevin's own inventive skills, he started work on his own version of the equipment.

After a lot of trial and error, he got it working. Paul was the camera person, so he had to become proficient in the use of the gadget, which took a lot of practice. It was a heavy piece of equipment, which involved a lot of strengthening exercises to be able to walk and film at the same time, so you'd see Paul roaming the streets with the camera attached to him, morning, noon and night.

Paul with Kevin's 'Steadicam'

The Crane

Tripod system

Blue Screen

When the technology of 'blue screen' came on the scene, Kevin became passionate about that too. He saw all the possibilities and learned as much as he could about it, a technology that would save him having to build sets or rent indoor locations. Every piece of equipment he needed, he started making. But first he had to find a suitable house where he could film, take the pictures home and recreate a 'blue screen house' in his studio. He constructed an enormous screen. One side was painted green and the other side was painted blue. The paint was special paint and he also found suitable furniture and painted that blue. We were surrounded by blue! He found a beautiful house in Wicklow Town and the owners were willing to allow him to film the interiors. In the end he ended up with a movie he was very happy with. And he sold it to several European TV stations.

Filming directly to Computer

Another of his go-ahead ideas was to film directly onto computer, instead of onto film or video tape. He designed a rig that we could take with us on location. It consisted of a hard drive and all the tech needed to record onto it. We shot two short films that way - 'Business Partners' and 'In the Same Boat'.

Seamus acting with Kevin in Kevin's comedy, 'Bob and Mary'

Hello Dolly

Kevin also make his own Camera Dolly, tracks and several different Cranes. With the camera mounted on the Crane, using his own home-made remote control, Kevin could focus the lens and also zoom, tilt and pan. On one of his films, which he made on location high up in the Kerry mountains in the south of Ireland, the crew had to haul the Crane all the way up the mountain. It was a huge undertaking and Kevin spared no expense in time and effort to get what he thought would be a fabulous shot. But, unfortunately, the weather turned very stormy and much of the footage couldn't be used.

Camera Dolly

Another time, while shooting in Killarney National Park near a waterfall, the actress had to fall into a deep pool of water, like a small lake, and be rescued by the lead actor. The actors were literally eaten alive by midges and, to make matters worse, a lot of grief was caused by a man who wanted to spend time exactly on the spot where we were filming. We had to wait for a couple of hours until he felt fully satisfied that he had seen all he wanted to see. He was very aggressive and wanted to discuss in depth why he had the right to be where he wanted, as this was a free country and he had come to pay this particular part of Kerry a visit. Eventually he moved on and Kevin got his shot. Oh brother!

**Location of the
'Kerry Pool
Experience'**

Kevin was supportive of films that other community members wanted to make. He had passed his passion onto everyone else in the community, so everybody started writing scripts and making productions in order to learn the trade. While in Roundstone, as well as having acting classes every day, we re-made scenes from several tv series that we liked, such as 'Private Benjamin' or 'Cagney and Lacey'. So everybody got a chance to learn how to shoot, direct, edit and act.

Me as 'Cagney'   **Veronica as 'Lacey'**

After we came to Wicklow, we made a film on Glendalough, a beautiful, ancient monastic site in Ireland, and called it 'Glendalough - A Mystical Journey'. It was shown quite a number of times on TV, and later was very successful as a VHS video and DVD.

Cover artwork
for
Glendalough
DVD

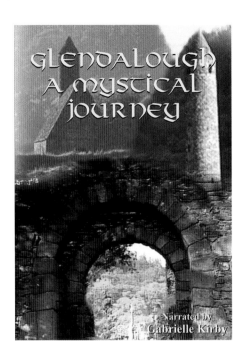

Kevin's set, Lough Dan, Co. Wicklow

Extras

Seamus as a decrepit hunchback

Kevin -
Dickensian clerk

To aid the filming process when we moved to Wicklow, we signed up with several agencies to be extras on any upcoming movie. In fact, some of our happiest memories are from the time we did 'extra work' on many different films.

The first movie we worked on was the Irish-made 'Guiltrip'. Because we were so interested in the filming process, we absorbed everything on the set - the way they set up the scenes, the directions they gave the actors, and then, of course, when we got a chance to do our bit we were very eager altogether. We were delighted to be chosen to be part of any scene. We were supplied all our meals - lunch, dinner, breaks, even dessert. We were totally surprised and delighted about dessert, one of the choices being Pavlova. Being in the community and never having dessert after our dinner, we were amazed that such a dessert even existed. it was such a pleasure! We were even more amazed that they actually paid us on the way home. Here we were doing something that we loved, eating food that we also loved and then, on top of that, getting paid for it. This was the life!

Other movies we were extras on were 'Moll Flanders' with Robin Wright and Morgan Freeman, 'The Laws of Attraction' with Pierce Brosnan and Julianne Moore, 'The Boxer' with Daniel Day Lewis, 'Kidnapped' with Armand Assante, 'The Abduction Club' with Paul Bettany, 'The Suicide Club' with Stephen Rea, 'Michael Collins' with Liam Neeson and Alan Rickman, 'The General' with Jon Voigt, 'Lassie' and many more.

Bernard   Me in the middle.   Seamus
                           Vera on the left.

Maura with Kevin
in
'The Magnificent
Ambersons'

The Mystic Knight

Kevin was in an American production called 'Mystic Knights', which was shot in Ardmore Studios, Co. Wicklow. It was winter and very cold. The outfit he had to wear was a tunic type top and thin tights. One time, on an extremely cold morning, as he was putting on his tights, he got the bright idea to put his tights over his trousers. This was the last straw for the girl in charge of costumes. She nearly had a fit! 'There's always one!' was her exasperated comment. It was such a great source of amusement for the community when he came home and told us about it. We laughed for ages. From then on, we would always tease him about it and to this day we still get a great laugh out of it.

Kevin always wore glasses, but during the takes on 'Mystic Knights' he was required to take them off. The ADs (assistant directors) were warned to watch out for anyone with glasses or anything that would take away from the authentic look of the film. Kevin would take his glasses off for the take and put them back on the second the take was over. After the take, when the AD looked across at Kevin, he would have his glasses on. The AD would make a beeline for him to ask him if he had them on during the take and Kevin would tell them he didn't. But they were never sure. Kevin was always so quick at putting them on after each take!

**Kevin the
'Mystic Knight'
without glasses
(thankfully!)**

Kevin hated to be idle. He loved working on new ideas. Consequently, he always had the latest gadget. Being interested in new, convenience technology, he wanted the smallest computer he could possibly get. His son, Mark, gave him a present of a small hand-sized computer, a PDA (Personal Digital Assistant). Kevin absolutely loved it and brought it everywhere with him. But it was soon superceded by a newer model, which Kevin wanted. It just happened to come out right at the time he was on the set of a movie as an extra. And, as he wasn't being used on set for some time, he asked for permission to go to town to buy the gadget. It was amazing, but he was actually given permission. Off he headed to town to buy the PDA. He bought it, arrived back and started working on it straight away. He was so focussed on what he was doing, trying to figure out how it worked, that he didn't even notice or hear the assistant director calling out his name to go on set. In fact, the AD passed behind him calling 'Jacobsen! Kevin Jacobsen!' as he sat all absorbed in his new gadget. Of course, Kevin was now a little hard of hearing, too, so he never as much as cast a glance in the AD's direction. That was one of the funniest episodes ever. I'm not even sure if Kevin was used at all that day. But he was one happy man with his brand new PDA.

Kevin's PDA

Kevin and I were on a film together called 'The Actors' with Michael Caine and because we both had health issues we brought all our own food and ate it together in the car when there were breaks. It was hard because we both love food, and especially the food they give you on the set. The menu on set would be quite different from what we were accustomed to, and, unfortunately, it might not be too healthy. But we stuck it out and were really glad when we got home that we hadn't partaken of the unhealthy fare. In fact, a lot of the attraction of being an extra was the food.

**Veronica
in
'Rebel Heart'**

**Michaela with
Liam Neeson and
Alan Rickman in
'Michael Collins'**

Kevin rented out our studio to Ardmore Studios who were making a film with James Spader. We got to meet him, and Vera (left) and myself had our photo taken with him.

We were also extras on 'Ballykissangel' and 'Fair City' several times.

Kevin appeared in 'The Laws of Attraction', 'The Clinic', 'David Copperfield', 'Mystics Knights', 'Durango', 'Michael Collins', 'The Magnificent Ambersons', 'The Mammy' and many more.

Vera, James Spader, Me

Kevin on set of
'Michael Collins'

Bernard and Michaela
in 'The Mammy'

Myself and Paul in 'Lassie'

Vera in
'Random Passage'

Always the Inventor

Kevin used to say that all you need when you are getting married is a roof over your head and a tea chest for a table and then, when you weren't using the table, it could act as a playpen for your kids. I remember when I first visited Kevin, his youngest boy, Philip, was in a square box which Kevin had made for him. What Kevin liked about it was the fact that if the baby wanted to play he would stand up and look over the top and when he wanted to be on his own he would sit or lie down in the box without everyone looking at him. He believed it was the perfect item for any baby and he really liked the idea of the freedom the baby had in his box. It was a big hit with his kids.

When Kevin had his cabinet-making business, he was also into motorbikes, and he would transport his newly-made furniture in a home-made sidecar.

When his kids were small, he had a box on the back of his motorbike and he used tp put them in it and Mary would sit in the sidecar. There were holes in the sides of the box so the kids could look out. They loved it! The neighbours didn't approve at all.

One year, when we were in the Legion of Mary, we travelled over to a Fleadh Cheoil in County Clare and Kevin had the sidecar full of cooking equipment and sleeping bags. When we reached our destination, we offloaded all the equipment and also the sidecar box. What was left was a frame attached to the motorbike that you could stand on. He transported us all to the field where the event was taking place, all standing on the platform. it was terrific! Otherwise we would have had to walk. But a Garda (Irish Policeman) gave us a gentle warning which put a stop to our fun transport.

He invented a super door-closer - a little bag of sand that was attached to the door by a rope through a set of pulleys. When you opened the door, the bag was pulled up, and after you went through, the weight of the sandbag caused the door to close. We had them on all our doors up to a few years ago.

Kevin's Wisdom Sayings

Kevin had a great deal of wisdom which he shared with us over the years. It became condensed into sayings and practices which we adhere to still.

Celebrate Failure

Weakness is one of the most talked about subjects in our community and it is largely because of Kevin and his love of weakness. He embraced his weakness and weaknesses in every way and it is still a big part of our community ethos.

One thing we lay a lot of emphasis on is the importance of celebrating failure. No matter what type of failure you have, you need to tell someone so that you can celebrate it. Not a celebration on your own, but a public celebration so that everyone gets to join in. By nature, we don't like to fail in any way. We despise failure. The reason behind the special celebration is to counteract the negative effect that failure has on ourselves and others. When we fail, we like to hide it or pretend it didn't happen, even beat ourselves up over it. But when we celebrate, we bring it out in the open, laugh at it and try to see the good that could come from it. And we get something nice to eat, too!

After all, failure is only postponed success.

Whatever you fail in, don't fail to become a saint.

Kevin was very impressed with the saints and the 'Science of the Saints'. He was always interested in becoming a saint. Not the miracle-working type, but simply a true Friend of God, which was his own definition. He was very impressed when he read the life of St. Bernard, how his father said to him that he could only make one mistake in life and that was not to become a saint. Kevin loved anything to do with the saints and had his favourites - the 'small' saints, the ones who didn't do fantastic things; 'small' in the sense of performing no miracles, who just did the ordinary things extraordinarily well. His favourite saint was St. Therese of Lisieux. He loved her 'little way' of offering everything to God, both good and bad. Everything pleasant and unpleasant could be offered as an act of love. It seemed, because of her great love, that God gave her everything she wanted.

Happy Am I

Kevin coined a beautiful phrase, 'Happy Am I', and used it very much in the last year of his life. He seemed to say it for anything that happened to him that he didn't care for, whether it was sickness, disappointment or whatever occurred that went against his nature in any way. I think he especially used it in relation to his heart condition. He liked to walk to Mass, but because of his angina he would have to stop many times and take a rest. He would use that time to look around and enjoy his surroundings. Then, when the pain subsided, he would move on again and take another few steps. He made his whole journey to the church, or when he would go out to write with his little computer, a whole experience of thanking God for whatever he would have to go through. To honour him, we had his favourite saying engraved on his gravestone. He has some beautiful writings on 'Happy Am I' which we've passed on to others, and many people use the saying in their own lives.

Avoid the 'Three Ds'

In the early days, we travelled around the country a lot trying to spread the faith. Our first job when we arrived in a new town was to look for somewhere to stay. Once we had that safe place to leave our belongings we could then go out on the street and approach the people and try to interest them in loving God.

Our first port of call in Ballybunion, Co. Kerry was the Convent of Mercy. The nuns welcomed us with open arms. They could not have been nicer to us. They brought us in and gave us a huge room to sleep in where we set up our sleeping bags. Then they brought us to their kitchen and gave us whatever we wanted to eat. In the evening, after our work on the streets, all the nuns joined with us and we talked together about our mission and what we hoped to accomplish.

Kevin, of course, was the centre of attention. The nuns were very interested in his story and how he became a Catholic. He became great friends with the mother superior, Mother Virgilius. She gave Kevin great encouragement in relation to talking about God to people and the great good it did. 'Even if you don't think it does anything at the time,' she said, 'afterwards, God's word would be buzzing in their ears.' One thing she also told him was to avoid the 'Three Ds' - the Doctor, the Devil and the Dumps. Kevin liked the simplicity of that and talked a lot about the 'Three Ds' down through the years.

I solemnly vow... only to see the Goodness of God in everything.

As Kevin says himself in his autobiography, he learned the habit of criticising. Criticising everything and everybody! One thing he didn't like to see was rubbish on the street or anywhere. I suppose, coming from Denmark, he wouldn't have been used to seeing rubbish anywhere at all, because everything in Denmark is extremely neat and tidy.

Because he had taken a vow to be positive, he couldn't really grumble about the rubbish anymore. So he trained himself to admire all the different colours. In that way he would distract himself from the awfulness of the sight and also from criticising the person or people who had caused the rubbish to be there in the first place. By highlighting in his mind the lovely colours he was seeing, he was also free from blaming himself for being so critical. And so he was able to preserve his peace of mind, which was always a priority for him.

Once, while he was in LA promoting his movies, he got on to the set of the TV series 'Mike Hammer' with actor Stacy Keach. They were beyond friendly to him. They actually thought he was a bishop. He was treated like a king. He loved it. In fact, he loved America. When he came back, he talked a lot about the freedom he experienced there. He never seemed to grumble or dwell on the fact that the minute he arrived in LA, his car was broken into and all his possessions were robbed!

So much that's better!

We got a lot of mileage out of Kevin's version of 'So much the better'. 'So much the better' came from the autobiography of St. Therese of Liseaux. When she had TB, the pain eventually became so unbearable that she wasn't able to thank God or utter any positive statement about her illness. So she asked her sisters to say to her 'So much the better', since she herself was only able to groan. Kevin was really very impressed with the fact that she had so much courage and audacity, and a complete understanding of weakness. In her weakened state, she knew she wouldn't be able to say anything positive. So she wanted her sisters to do it for her.

We had a lot of fun with Kevin about this, because, being Danish, I suppose, he wasn't able to say it correctly. He was so magnanimous not to get hurt by our constant joking with him over it. His way of saying it was 'So much that's better'. He would say it himself and also suggested that we say it too if something got too hard to bear. It was like having a complete contempt for your own pain, offering it to God so He could use it to save souls.

Kevin's Funny Sayings

Living in Inishere probably had the biggest influence on Kevin. He was always talking about Inishere and especially about all the things they said and got up to. Just about everything you could possibly think up about Inishere he would talk about. Constantly. There's nothing we don't know about his time there. Consequently, we love the island just as much as he did, if that's possible.

Occasionally, when it was a bit breezy, Kevin might begin to talk about the *Firrelvind*. We hadn't a clue what he was talking about, or whether this was a Danish or Irish word. For years, we just did not know what he was referring to. Eventually we found out that he was talking about a 'whirlwind', pointing out how it would make the leaves go round and round. He seemed to be always fascinated by the power of the wind to make things 'dance around in a circle'.

Because Kevin was Danish he had sayings that were really funny. When he was hungry, he would say he had *itchy teeth*. Or if he had something to eat and wasn't fully satisfied he would say, *'That went into my hollow tooth'*. He loved having fun. He must have picked that up on Inishere because they were always playing games and tricks on each other.

We loved to ask him to say Volkswagen. He would say *'Woltsvagon'*, and we would have a great laugh at his expense. But he didn't mind. If he ate something and it was tasteless, his expression was *'It's like sticking the tongue out the window'*. When something got caught in his throat and he had to cough it up he would say, *'It went down the wrong throat'*. If you had to do something that demanded courage, he would say, *'Grab the bull by the horn'*.

Epilogue

After Kevin and Veronica came back from their visit to the USA, Kevin felt an urge to visit Denmark. Denmark was not one of his favourite places, although he did have a lot of friends there who had come to visit him in Ireland occasionally. His friend, Alan Thuesen and his wife, Kirsten, would come nearly every year and spend their summer holidays with us in the community.

Kevin went to Denmark with three things in mind. He was putting together a book on his life, so he wanted to get all the facts right. He wanted to revisit all the places of his youth where he grew up, meet old friends and visit cake shops in Copenhagen where he could gather recipes for the restaurant he was going to open. Veronica went along, too. On his return, his former opinion of Denmark had changed. He now felt very warm towards his native country and had enjoyed the company of his brother and wife, and his friends. And he was especially happy with all the fabulous photos he had taken of extraordinary cakes and, of course, the food-tasting went down very well, too!

In the beginning of July he wasn't feeling very well and I was going to Spain with Seamus. We were performing at a music festival in Oviedo, in the north of Spain. We were a little concerned about Kevin being sick, so when I was leaving I said to him, 'Don't go anywhere when I'm gone.' He replied, 'I've no intention of going anywhere.' I was happy with that. But, while in Spain, we got a phone call to say that Kevin was in a critical condition. He had found it difficult to breathe and the doctor came to see him. An ambulance was called and he was taken to nearby Loughlinstown hospital, where they were going to put a stent in his heart. Maura and Vera accompanied him on his journey. Before he had the operation he said to them, 'Don't come in tomorrow because I'll probably be too groggy. Come in the next day.' Then, prior to surgery, they found he was in a more critical condition than formerly thought and sent him to St. James's hospital in Dublin. During the operation, they found that his heart was too badly damaged to withstand a by-pass.

In the meantime, Seamus and I returned home to be with him. He was in ICU, kept alive on machines. We all went in to see him every day for a week. His sons also visited him. Sadly, Mary was unable to make the journey. The doctors told us there was no hope, that he wouldn't pull through, but he looked so peaceful. Each member of the community spent some time with him alone, a personal way of saying goodbye. I felt sure that when they took him off the machines that he would just come round. I guess God had other plans. On the Friday of that week, we got a call from St. James's hospital to say that we should all come in. We contacted his sons and we all met at the hospital.

We were all sitting around his bed at about 1am in the morning, the time we usually sing the Psalms, so we sang our night Psalms and then said the Rosary. I spoke privately with Kevin's eldest son, Louis, and we both agreed, in discussion with Kevin's doctor, that it was time to turn off the machines. When they switched off the life support, Kevin took about three breaths and then went to his heavenly home.

It was so hard to believe that he was actually gone from our lives. Everything centred around Kevin. But we had to move on. Kevin had laid a great foundation for us. Through him we had been exposed to so many different experiences. We learned to fish with hand lines, how to use all sorts of machines, we built the longline system from scratch. We ran a rope-making business, a machine workshop. We learned how to write, produce and edit movies. We learned how to play music, produce CDs and DVDs. We've been on the radio, TV, given talks, concerts, retreats.

Kevin was buried on his beloved Inishere, in a beautiful corner of the graveyard overlooking Galway Bay. Two years later, Mary died. She is buried alongside him. Two great souls!

I hope they are smiling down on us now, happy with the work we are doing, encouraging us to carry on the legacy of seeing and preaching the Goodness of God in everything.

**The author at Kevin's and Mary's graves
on Inishere**

Vow of the Positive

Here is the text of the 'Vow of the Positive', as we call it for short. Kevin composed it to help himself and us remain positive about all the things that occur in our lives. The 'positive' is based on the fact that God is infinitely good and always looking after our wellbeing. If we trust in His goodness and stay positive, it gives Him the freedom to look after us with great care. The community renews this vow to Our Lady every year on 25th March, her feast day.

The Vow of Seeing God's Goodness in Everything

One of the wonderful things with the vow is that it reveals how good God is and how much He loves everyone of us.

The revelation of His goodness will be in discovering a whole new world of beauty within yourself, and a beauty all around you. You are now no longer driven by the fear of God, but love Him because of His goodness.

Because man has been given free will, you may at times witness people choosing that which is not positive, refusing to see the goodness and mercy of God, but even in witnessing that you can still rejoice in the fact that God in His goodness gave us the freedom to choose, that freedom which is so essential to the process of loving.

Taking this vow means always and ever to interpret everything you see and hear in the light of God's goodness and, because of that, God will show you that everything is perfect in this imperfect world.

The vow will help you discover how God protects you against the awareness of evil, and the discouragement of failure. And He will constantly show you more and more the beautiful wonders of life.

As you go along you will begin to treasure the vow more than anything else in your life, and you will not fear to proclaim that you have made this solemn vow. And should you repeatedly experience negativity from a person, you would, out of loyalty to your vow, enlighten the person that you cannot serve two masters, the positive and the negative.

Finally, take it as an honour if you, due to your vow, in any way appear foolish or gullible, or have to endure some humiliation for the great privilege and grace of preferring to see the Goodness of God in every little thing.

The Vow

I.......................... solemnly vow to you my dearest mother that I will choose forever and always, from now on until the end of my life, only to see the Goodness of God in everything.

Let it be life or death, peace or war, the greatest success or total ruin, I promise only to think positively, speak positively, listen positively and look with a positive vision, until the day I die.

When I vow to you my dearest mother, I vow with all my heart, with all my strength and with everything I am, never to go back on my vow of only seeing God's Goodness in everything.

Should I, through human weakness, fail to be positive I will instantly undo my failure by adding something positive which will result in my continuing to see the glorious, wonderful beauty of the Goodness of God. Amen.

Arne Jacobsen
Kevin's father

Jokum, Mary
and Kevin

Alan and Kirsten
Thuesen with
Kevin

Mary

Louis, Me, Jacob
(Kevin's nephew)
& Aoife (my sister)
with her baby